GOD STORIES

Renewing Your Faith in the One
Who Hears Every Prayer

By Courtney Dailey

Unless otherwise noted, Scripture quotations are taken from the ESV® Bible (The Holy Bible, English Standard Version®), © 2001 by Crossway, a publishing ministry of Good News Publishers. Used by permission. All rights reserved.

ISBN 979-8-218-74978-1

Editing by Deirdre Lockhart of Brilliant Cut Editing
Cover art © by Muhammad Arslan. Used by permission.

This work is based on true events,
a work of creative nonfiction.
While the stories in this book are true and
portrayed to the best of Courtney Dailey's memory,
she may not have remembered precise dialogue
or exact descriptions of certain things.
These stories were retold with the intention
of evoking the emotion
and meaning behind each event.
Some names and identifying specifics
have been changed to protect
the privacy of individuals involved.

To watch the original videos documenting this
miraculous story,
follow Courtney on her Facebook page:
Author Courtney Dailey.

To subscribe to her free weekly newsletter,
check out Dailey's Weekly on Substack.

To My Husband, Paul

For the countless times you dried my tears

and told me to keep going,

prayed my worries to silence,

or encouraged me to chase the impossible...

You are my rock. Thank you, sweetheart.

I love you.

CHAPTER ONE

I blinked several times. This wasn't the street I remembered. Debris littered the shattered asphalt beneath my tires. This was like the scene of a science fiction movie, not real life. Household items, tossed and rolled in mud, lay in silent, reckless abandon. Toys. Clothing. Towels. Remnants of cars and furniture. Trees. Power lines.

Water had done *this*?

"Mom…" my nine-year-old daughter whispered. She covered her open mouth with one hand.

I could only nod.

I scanned the area where my friend Jerry's garage used to be, his favorite hangout. Nothing remained save its concrete slab. Next to it perched his old Jeep, cockeyed and muddy, like a toy car a boy played with in the creek and then forgot. Grass and tree limbs clung to its broken windows. If the garage was nowhere in sight, had Jerry been swept away too?

One crushed and mangled house was parked sideways in the creek in his front yard. Its glassless windows stared back at us. His property was a land mine of random belongings—appliances, bent metal, someone's patio chair, and mud. Sand. River silt.

Then I spotted Jerry.

He was standing in the muck in his neighbor's yard. I thrust the gearshift into park, engine still running, and my daughter and I jumped out, racing to his side. He hugged us both, and we cried, the reunion too heavy for words.

Worried about him, my husband and I tried contacting Jerry for two days. The storm had knocked out all cell service. The last news we'd received of his whereabouts was from a Facebook post forty-eight hours before. As the water rose in his yard, he'd shared photos.

Jerry was a longtime friend. We'd adopted him into our family some ten years before. Now, he came to most of our holiday gatherings and celebrations.

"I'm so thankful you're okay." I told him once we stopped crying.

He shook his head, his lower lip trembling. "Everything is gone."

"What about your house?" I sucked in a deep breath. "Can it be saved?"

Beyond him, the 967-square-foot home was still awkwardly propped on its foundation. A waterline marked its exterior at least five feet above the floor. The siding was a canvas of finger-painted mud. Every broken window was curtained in leaves and tree limbs.

"I'll show you." He took my arm, his hand shaky. His tennis shoes with no socks slogged through muck at least a foot deep.

Then it started to rain.

"Do you have boots?" I tugged up my raincoat hood.

"I have nothing." He lowered his head, and new tears spotted his dirty T-shirt. His eyes carried the heavy despair of someone with no hope. No direction.

My heart twisted.

As we rounded the back of his house, the gravity of Jerry's situation revealed itself. An angry wall of water had plowed down Clearwater Street, without warning, carrying homes, trees, and vehicles. The current had ripped through Jerry's bedroom window and left in its wake a five-foot-deep pile of branches and muck.

We weren't standing in a bedroom doorway, but in a tangled, overgrown beaver dam. When the rapids had nothing more to eat, they'd torn west, taking Jerry's entire back wall with them.

What remained was a frail dollhouse, opened on a hinge with the contents exposed.

Except few contents were left.

In those destructive moments, the rapids snatched nearly all of Jerry's belongings. Every piece of his family's antique furniture was obliterated. His clothes dryer remained where it had settled, now a living room focal piece. The washing machine was nowhere to be found. His side-by-side refrigerator lay on its back in the middle of the kitchen, concreted in place in two feet of brown sludge. His deep freezer was gone. Even his propane tank was missing. A single red toddler shoe sparkled on his porch steps. Who knew how many miles it had traveled to get here.

I blinked, swallowing another onslaught of tears. "Where were you when this happened?"

"I was in my garage." He pointed back toward the slab. His hand was still trembling. "The water rose within a matter of seconds. When I saw it coming down the street, I jumped into my Honda. But by the time I backed out of my driveway, the water was up to my windshield. I just started praying because I knew this was it. I was going home to be with Jesus. And then... my car floated to higher ground where EMS was waiting."

I raised my eyebrows. "Your car... floated to higher ground, right where EMS was waiting?"

He nodded.

"Cars don't float, Jerry."

"I know. It was the Lord." He spread his fingers on both hands. "That's the only explanation."

As we walked away from the house, I checked my phone to see if I could call my husband, Paul. Of course there was still no service. Paul had gone to the Hampton Fire Department with his excavator to see how he might help other flood victims in the area. We needed his excavator here. We needed twenty excavators. And skid steers. And dump trucks.

We needed a miracle.

"Let's go into town and see if we can find you some boots and a rain jacket." I patted Jerry's arm. "And you're coming to our house. Have you eaten?"

"No." He backed away a step in the slosh. "A friend's letting me stay in the upstairs apartment next to his house. It's just a block away. I have to stay close to keep an eye on things."

"What do you mean?" I waved to the destruction. What was there to keep an eye on? Most of his belongings were either washed away or soiled beyond repair.

"The looters come out at night and steal things," he explained, his gaze dark.

"Are you serious?" I clenched my jaw.

People were lurking around this neighborhood, snatching the last bits and pieces of these residents' lives? Tears burned my view again as I peered down the street. There were countless damaged homes. A parade of flipped vehicles dotted the landscape. Lost and hurting people, their faces ghostly, stood planted in their yards, surveying the ruin. Volunteers in all-terrain vehicles handed out waters and bags of food.

"Come on. Get in my car," I ordered. "Let's take you out of here for a bit."

He didn't want to come along because of the mud on his shoes. I wagged my head. The cleanliness of my floormats didn't matter. Obviously. Nothing mattered. The people on this street had lost everything.

I insisted on a pit stop at Walmart first, so we could pick up basic necessities. The flood in Hampton, Tennessee, resulted from a cruel thirty inches of rainfall Hurricane Helene dumped two days before. The historic floodwaters charged in thunderous raging rapids from the mountains and into our county's valleys. But as we departed the small community of Hampton and drove back into the city of Elizabethton, the electricity was already restored. Restaurants were open. Life was eerily normal.

Jerry didn't want to go shopping, so he stayed in the car. We had a list: a coat, rubber boots (size 10), socks, sweatpants, and sweatshirts. Plus, Jerry needed the simple everyday stuff like a toothbrush, pillow, and soap. He requested ice trays too for the apartment where he was staying.

My daughter and I loaded up a cart with everything we could find on the list, except the boots. We saved those for last. Honestly, I knew they were a lost cause. Then we turned onto the shoe aisle to empty shelves in the wake of the disaster. Just like I figured.

"God, please let us find him some boots," I prayed. But there were no rubber boots left in any size. They must've been cleaned out in the last two days. Everyone needed boots to contend with the mud. I couldn't find ice trays either.

With our buggy full, we headed to the checkout. It was getting late, and I still needed to convince Jerry to eat with us. He was a diabetic. I could only imagine he wasn't taking care of himself.

"Mom, look!" My daughter pointed to a display of ice trays at one of the endcaps.

"That's a weird spot for ice trays." I snagged a set and checked that item off my list. "Let's get out of here."

We turned down the aisle for self-checkout and strolled past a shelf of clearance office supplies. And there on the bottom, between paper and pens and organizers, waited one lone pair of black rubber boots. The only pair of rubber boots I'd seen in the entire store. I reached for them and flipped over the tag. Men's, size 10.

"Thank you, God," I whispered through my closing throat and placed them in the buggy.

We convinced Jerry to go eat with us at the Italian restaurant in town. Glassy-eyed, he confessed he hadn't eaten in two days. After we ordered, I folded my hands in my lap to keep from reaching for his still shaky ones. "Do you have flood insurance?"

His family home was paid for. He'd lived there most of his nearly seventy years.

He dropped his chin, and the corners of his eyes creased. "No. But maybe homeowner's insurance will cover something?"

I shrugged. "I have no idea."

And we still didn't have cell service, so we couldn't just Google it.

"You reckon I'll have to tear my house down?" His eyes widened.

I pursed my lips together. With the foundation damage on the back of his house, how could we save it? But I wouldn't say that.

He must've read my expression before I could school it. His jawbone flexed. "Courtney, I can't go anywhere else. I've lived there my whole life. Hampton is my home."

"I know. Maybe we can put you in a camper until a new house can be built?" But I had no idea what I was talking about. I was grasping for anything to reassure him, to lessen the devastation in his eyes.

My husband was a builder and a contractor. Although we had our retail store endeavor, most of our livelihood came from building and flipping homes during the four years we'd been married. He'd have answers and know what to do. I couldn't wait to get home and talk to him... if he was home. How strange not being able to communicate with anyone.

A man approached our table and put his hand on Jerry's shoulder. "I heard about your house."

Jerry's eyes filled again. "I'm alive. I'm blessed. God's been good to me."

The man teared up too. "Well, we're praying for you."

After our dinner, the server informed us someone had paid for our meal. Jerry and I shared a tearful glance. Then I drove him back to his house.

"I can't believe you're still driving that Honda," I said as I turned and followed his street.

"Well, since I floated away, it gets stuck in second gear now. But I can drive it in the immediate area anyway."

He'd lost five vehicles in the flood, total. His hobby was working on old cars, several of them expensive classics he'd spent years fixing up. But he never actually drove them around town, so he hadn't carried insurance on them. Just one more loss he was grieving.

When we parked at the edge of his driveway, a man on a bicycle held a flashlight, searching piles of scattered belongings. A looter. I wasn't the confrontational type, but I sprang from my car, stood in the middle of the street, and screamed at the man to leave. How unfathomable to think someone would venture into an area of devastation and prey on the detriment of storm victims.

"We'll be back tomorrow, Jerry," I promised. "First thing in the morning, we'll help clean up, and we'll figure this out."

Jerry could only shake his head and cry.

Then I sobbed all the way home.

CHAPTER TWO

I felt guilty parking in my garage that night with the house lights burning bright. Not only did we have electricity, we had Wi-Fi too, which meant we could check messages and communicate with the outside world. We had a working kitchen and a fully stocked refrigerator. The beds were all adorned with multiple pillows. Our closets were crammed full of clothing, everything we needed. As I entered the bedroom, Paul was sitting against our headboard, scrolling through his phone.

I wanted to recount Jerry's whole story, but I couldn't talk. Instead, I fell into Paul's arms and cried. Once I'd caught my breath, I explained everything: Jerry's mauled house, temporary housing, and lack of flood insurance.

"Can we rebuild his house, Paul?" I hiccupped. "Is there any way?"

My husband, the eternal optimist and go-getter, shrugged. "I mean, I can look at it, and we'll see what we can do. But you're talking a hundred grand at least, honey."

"He has nothing." I sobbed, wiping my nose. "No savings. No flood insurance."

"Maybe FEMA will help him, but rumor is they're out of money."

I'd heard that too.

"We have to rebuild his house, Paul. We have to. I don't know what he's going to do. Couldn't we get volunteers or something? We have to get him back in. Winter is coming. He only has a temporary place to stay...."

"I know." My husband snuggled me in closer and prayed aloud as my tears fell on his T-shirt. "God, You know our hearts are breaking for our friend. And You know we want to help him. There are so many hurting right now. We can't afford to rebuild his house, but we want to do what we can. We need You to help us, God.... If there's any way

You can send us what we need to rebuild this community, we need You. Let us get Jerry back in his house by Christmas."

The prayer went on for fifteen minutes, and I cried through most of it. Neither of us slept well that night.

The next morning, I woke both of our kids bright and early. It was Monday, three days after the flood. Schools were closed for the next couple of weeks. This part of the country was on pause. Nothing felt routine.

When the kids asked what we were doing, I explained, "We're going to help Jerry."

We dressed in old clothes and rubber boots. Then we loaded up my car and Paul's truck with snow shovels and work gloves. My husband hauled a trailer with his mini excavator and followed us into Hampton.

Jerry was already there when we arrived. We all hugged him, and he cried again as he told Paul how God had spared his life as he was carried off in the floodwaters. The street was quiet today, desolate.

My husband fired up his excavator and began clearing debris from the yard. The kids and I went to Jerry's house, but even taking one step was difficult with the mud so deep. We started a pile in the backyard of things we thought we could salvage, plus family heirlooms and photo albums. The mood was solemn and quiet. Jerry sat in a camping chair by the road, staring at the mountains, unable to watch.

The house smelled like sewage and rotten food. My heart shattering, I collected slimy framed pictures of family members and wet and ruined drawers full of old Christmas cards and letters. There were water-damaged antiques and piles of grimy, earth-smeared clothes. We discarded broken dishes. Jerry's prized KitchenAid mixer on the counter was under water, plug and all.

The electric company had come through and pulled every meter on the street so cleanup could begin with no fire hazards.

Then came the rumbling of more engines. Beyond the cruddy windows, lines of heavy equipment barreled down the street. A blonde lady in a white dump truck hauled mountains of debris from my husband's excavator. And then there were more excavators. And skid steers. And more dump trucks. They were all locals, driving into Hampton with fuel and machinery to see how they could help for the day.

Someone spoke from the open front door.

I jolted.

A crew of six or seven people stood there in rubber boots, shovels in hand.

"Are you Courtney?" a lady asked.

"I am."

"Jerry said you were in charge. Tell us what to do."

I gave a silent no. "Well, I don't know about being in charge, but we're trying to sort what can be saved and shovel mud out of the rest of the house."

"Great. We'll get started." She gave a chipper wave and scooted off.

Soon over a dozen of us shoveled mud out of the house. All perfect strangers. We worked together, dumping mud through the open windows. The loads were heavy, the work exhausting, and the stench awful. But no one seemed to mind. No one complained.

We were a unified force, just grateful to help in some way, and we made good progress. Within two hours, we'd shoveled out the entire house, removed furniture, and salvaged items onto trucks. More volunteers would do their best to rinse off the muck in their own homes and see what could be saved.

With the mucking out finished, two men showed up from Jerry's church with pressure washers. Someone else arrived and rigged up the water line from the road so we could run a hose. Another crew with skid steers and excavators began tearing down the broken house in Jerry's creek bed.

All the while, Jerry sat by the edge of the road, a blank stare on his face. Someone brought a cooler with waters and Gatorade. Someone else showed up with snacks.

"Do you want something to eat?" Jerry offered.

But I couldn't eat. I didn't want to.

While the kids grabbed a granola bar, I chugged a bottle of water.

Besides the guys pressure washing inside the house, there was nothing else to do. And it was only lunchtime.

"Well, I guess we'll tear out the drywall and insulation tomorrow," I told Jerry.

He frowned. "I've heard we're not supposed to touch the house or anything until we hear from insurance or FEMA."

"I took pictures and videos." I downed another gulp, secretly terrified we'd done the wrong thing. What if FEMA *did* come in and tell us they wouldn't help because we'd cleaned up the mess? What if Jerry's homeowner's insurance wouldn't come through because we'd altered the disaster site?

I changed the subject. "I wish we had a crew to help us go ahead and rip out this insulation and drywall today, so we could bring in fans and get the house dried out."

As if they'd heard me, a dozen women came into view, walking down the street. They all wore Isaiah House T-shirts. Isaiah House was the local charity providing refuge for children awaiting foster care placement.

I nudged Jerry. "You think they would want to help us?"

"Do you have any tools?" He blinked at me like I'd lost my mind.

"Nope."

He laughed. "Courtney, how are you going to rip out drywall and insulation with no tools?"

"I don't know."

Jerry called to one lady he knew. "Would your group like to help?"

"Sure!" they shouted back. But they weren't wearing mud boots, and some of them didn't even have gloves.

"We'll do anything you need," the lady assured him as they drew nearer.

"Courtney will tell you what to do." Jerry gave me a look.

It seemed he thought I would instantly know. Sure, my husband and I build and flip houses, but I don't actually *do* most of the work. I've helped some on demo, and I ride around with him a lot, mostly hanging out on jobsites. But I'm no construction worker or carpenter. Of course, I didn't have to be a carpenter to do demolition. I was far from qualified to be in charge, though.

"All the drywall and insulation has to come out." I led the group along, and we all packed into Jerry's little house. The air was humid, and I was already sweating.

"How do we do that?" someone asked.

"Uh... With anything you can find." I picked up a curtain rod and handed it over.

She studied it.

We all got to work then, using our bare hands or kicking in the walls to break drywall and rip out insulation. What a crumbling, nasty mess!

We tossed the debris out the open back of the house. And wouldn't you know it? Some guy showed up on a tractor and began clearing the insulation and drywall as the piles grew.

Work crews were busy up and down the street all day. Mounds of debris doubled and then tripled in size. Excavators and dump truck operators created systems to clear the mess. A church nearby offered to let them dump everything in their adjacent empty lot until we could figure out what to do next, since volunteers weren't permitted to dump storm debris in the local landfill. By early afternoon, leaders emerged from groups of strangers who didn't know each other before, directing traffic and helping one another, coordinating the volunteer efforts.

Jerry appeared in the front doorway while we ripped out drywall. "Courtney, this man here is a contractor." He pointed his thumb to a man behind him. He wore a contractor T-shirt and held a nail gun at his side. "He's going to check the house and see if it can be saved."

"Okay. Great." I shook the man's hand.

Then he busied himself, climbing all over the house and nailing two-by-fours into place, testing the concrete blocks along the back wall's foundation.

The drywall job, admittedly, was nearly impossible. Jerry was right. We needed tools. This entire houseful of women had drywall in our hair, and muddy insulation clung to our clothing. Drenched in sweat, we persisted.

"I wish I had a crowbar," I told the lady working next to me. We were bumping elbows, clawing out drywall pieces in Jerry's tiny bathroom. I balanced on the edge of the sink while attempting to work near the ceiling.

"I saw one in the front yard!" someone called from the kitchen.

No way. I stopped what I was doing, climbed down, and headed that direction. "A ladder would be nice too," I joked as I came through the living room.

"Oh! There's a ladder too!" someone else said.

Seriously?

When I searched the front yard, I didn't find just one crowbar. I found three. And I found a ladder too. They were lying in the mud, right there together, like God had placed them in the exact spot we would see them. Funny. I hadn't noticed them before.

As soon as I climbed the ladder and began ripping more drywall out of the bathroom, a man's voice called from the side door.

"Hey! You guys need tools?" he asked.

"Yes!" we all yelled in unison.

"I've got tools! Hang on!" He went to his truck and came back with more crowbars, hammers, and screwdrivers. He brought his entire family too. The man explained they were from the next town over and they'd just driven in for the day to see how they could help.

Dawn had broken that morning in silence with a solemn understanding of the great loss. But by afternoon, everyone in Jerry's house was sharing God stories, quoting Scripture, and helping one another. An air of hope buoyed us, like these folks in Hampton might just be okay after all.

Then the contractor beckoned me to step off to the side.

"This house can be saved." He wiped his brow.

I grabbed this perfect stranger, yanked him into a bear hug, and cried some more.

He just laughed awkwardly. Then we went to tell Jerry.

By the end of the day, Jerry's entire house was gutted and pressure washed. All that remained was a roof, most of his foundation, and a partial skeleton of sided two-by-fours.

Trucks had hauled away the majority of the displaced house in the front yard. Bit by bit, we organized the mess into piles. And though the street still resembled a war zone, courage and unity shone in the eyes of every flood survivor and volunteer.

As I drove home that night, with dried mud lodged under my fingernails, I couldn't stop crying. But they weren't tears for the material things Jerry lost. I cried for the resiliency and strength of the area-wide strangers coming together, helping one another. I'd watched so many families and church groups in Jesus T-shirts pouring onto the street that day.

I'd gotten some mud in my eye during the muck-out phase, so I doused my face with a water bottle sometime midafternoon. I smelled awful. And of course, drywall crumbs dressed my hair.

But none of that mattered. The closeness I felt to God that evening was unlike anything I'd ever experienced. He'd been there with us throughout the workday, His presence a stronger force than I'd felt in any worship service at any church my entire life. God was *there*, walking alongside us. And He was showing us He cared.

Answering our prayers.

It reminded me of the verse in Psalm 34:18: "The Lord is near to the brokenhearted and saves the crushed in spirit."

As I parked in our garage, I directed my kids to go inside. I wanted to sit in my car and make a video about God's provisions in Hampton... the way He'd shown up for us again and again, the entire day. I only had six hundred followers on my Author Courtney Dailey Facebook page. I was a nobody. But I hoped maybe others would see what God was doing and they'd want to join in too. I wanted them to feel and experience the miracles I'd witnessed. Honestly, I couldn't keep it to myself. I needed to tell someone.

So I made the worst video I'd ever produced, ugly-crying as I sobbed through the God stories of the day. I told about the countless volunteers, the way every tool or piece of machinery had shown up exactly when we needed it—how food had been delivered the instant we said we were hungry, how God had sent us a plumber and a contractor in the very moment we needed them. I included video footage and pictures of Jerry's property. Then I posted it.

That night, my husband and I prayed again for the flood victims and how we might serve them, how we might somehow find a way to build back Jerry's house. And that night, again, sleep eluded us. Our souls raged with angst and uncertainty for our neighbors. The new burden for restoration weighed heavy on our hearts.

CHAPTER THREE

We continued our relief work in Hampton on Tuesday and Wednesday. My husband cleared debris while I coordinated efforts at Jerry's house. No government officials had made an appearance yet, though we heard FEMA was somewhere in the area. We stayed on the lookout every day, anxious for a contact with reliable information. Rumors rebounded about whether or not help was on the way.

We did learn one concerning fact, however. None of Jerry's homeowner's insurance covered flood damage. He would receive a few thousand dollars at most for his Honda Accord, which had officially stopped running. In the meantime, one of his friends loaned him a vehicle to drive.

Tuesday night after we got home, Paul and I both checked our phones. There was still no service. Only Wi-Fi. When I opened Facebook, I gasped.

"Paul! That video I made has six thousand views!" I grabbed his arm, squealing. "A lot of local people are asking how they can help, and they're volunteering to come down and do whatever they can!"

"Six thousand?" He gaped. "You've never had that many views!"

"I know! It's crazy! Maybe this will help get the word out." I started crying as I read through message after message.

"Maybe so."

As we said our bedtime prayers that night, we thanked God for the people messaging me, the people the Lord was already sending to help us. Our hearts exploded with gratitude. God was busy, making provisions and answering prayers.

The next morning, sleepy-eyed and sore all over, I stumbled into the bathroom to get ready. I checked the video to see if views had picked up overnight, and my eyes bulged. Chills raced up my arms. The video was up to seventeen thousand views. My heart pounded as the numbers climbed every minute. The notifications on the top of my screen were lighting up in constant succession. By the time I finished getting ready, the video had hit forty thousand views.

By 10:00 a.m., it was over a hundred thousand views. My phone was dinging every single second with thousands of messages from people all over the United States and then from all over the world, asking how they could help rebuild Jerry's house.

There were messages from Australia, Hawaii, Ireland, and Thailand.

I couldn't stop crying or thanking God. This was nothing but an answer to prayers. I was dying to tell Jerry, but of course there was no way to call him. I drove eagerly into Hampton, wailing and offering prayers of praise and thanksgiving the whole way. Jerry wasn't on his property. There was no choice but to circle the area, searching for him. I wasn't sure of the address where he was staying. Finally, I met him on the road and flashed my lights, signaling for him to pull over.

I barely got the car in park before I jumped out and ran at him, sobbing and screaming, "Jerry! You know that video I made about your house? It's had over a hundred thousand views. People from all over the world are messaging me! They want to rebuild your house. They're *going to rebuild* your house! You're going to have a home again!"

We stood on the roadside, cars whizzing past, bawling and hugging and jumping up and down like two excited children. We laughed maniacally, and then we cried again, literally screaming in wonder at what God was doing.

"I have no idea what to do now." I put my hands on my head. "Let's go to the bank and get their advice."

We drove to Carter County Bank and met with the president and a manager, who helped us set up a special account just for the rebuilding funds. Trying to get it all worked out without internet was a nightmare. I ended up driving home and working from my computer while on the phone with the bank. Then I decided to use my Venmo and transfer the money, which was also a nightmare. Within twenty-four hours, I had another thousand messages from all over the United States and six thousand in donations in my Venmo.

I called my church secretary, Lori, in a panic. This didn't feel right. It wasn't going to work this way.

"This is way bigger than me. Or Jerry's house. And I don't know what to do. Can we set up a special fund through the church to rebuild?" I asked. "I can't have all these people sending money to me, personally. It looks sketchy, and it makes me nervous. We want God to get the glory for this."

"I think we can set it up," she told me. She spoke to the elders, and they worked out a plan right away so God's family could donate directly through Central Community Christian Church.

We named the link the Save Jerry's House Fund, and I transferred the money from my Venmo to the new account. The donations poured in beyond anything we could have imagined.

I kept repeating that verse in my head, over and over again: "Now to Him who is able to do far more abundantly than all that we ask or think, according to the power at work within us, to Him be glory in the church and in Christ Jesus throughout all generations, forever and ever. Amen" (Ephesians 3:20–21).

That whole week, we worked in Hampton during the day and headed home at dark. Once I was connected to our home Wi-Fi, I spent hours going through messages, replying to folks who wanted to help. Someone out of California wanted to donate flooring for Jerry's home. Someone out of Georgia pledged not only to provide but also to install insulation and drywall. A lady in Maryland donated the bathroom vanities for his house. And countless church groups and work crews wanted to come in just to rebuild.

Doe River Gorge in Hampton offered to house volunteers at their camp for free. One of the directors from Doe River Gorge helped coordinate the efforts and worked on homes up and down the street.

Youth groups traveled in to muck out houses and crawl spaces. Once two volunteer veterans from Knoxville removed Jerry's siding, we discovered most of the band around his house was rotten. A local construction company donated their framing crew for the next week to get his home closed in, "back in the dry."

Each morning we set out to work on Clearwater Street, God furnished every supply. The first day our framing crew showed up to work on Jerry's house, one carpenter came to me and said, "We need twenty-seven sheets of subfloor."

"Just wait." I tucked my lower lip between my teeth, trying not to grin. "God will provide."

The crew leader raised one eyebrow and scratched his chin. But I'd been watching God work for over a week. I knew what He would do.

I pressed my hand to my heart. "Since we started this, God has sent us what we needed every single day."

In the meantime, now that we had cell service again, I called around to see where we might find subflooring and how much it would cost us.

Jerry stepped onto the porch. "Are you guys hungry?"

Churches and organizations brought breakfast, lunch, and dinner every day. Sometimes individuals came in their vehicles, handing out treat bags of snacks for the workers too. And of course, others brought in cases of Gatorade and water each day. One day, when our generator ran out of gas, we made a cardboard sign that said, "Need gas." An hour later, we came back, and every gas can was full.

"Yeah. Give me just a sec." I kept scrolling through my phone. "I have to find subfloor."

"Oh, hey." He tapped my arm. "I forgot to tell you. A deacon from my church said there are twenty-six sheets of subfloor in the church gym. Someone donated them. He said they're mine if I want them."

The framers stopped what they were doing, glancing at each other.

When their eyes found mine, I could only smile at them through my tears.

The entire week, when someone needed a drill or a charger, a stranger would pull up or walk into the yard and hand them what they needed. When our stomachs growled, food appeared. When we readied to order another building material, God sent the item or the funds to meet the demand.

On the third day of rebuilding, one worker stepped up to me. "We're going to need ninety-eight more two-by-fours."

"Ninety-eight?" I balked. That was a lot. Jerry's house wasn't big.

"Yeah," he explained. "Most of the wood is original, and a lot of it is rotten. If it hadn't been for the flood and all this rebuilding, his house would have collapsed in two or three years, tops."

I swallowed the lump in my throat. What would Jerry have done then? If his house had collapsed in two or three years, where would the help have come from? Would he have had any chance to rebuild? God had used the devastation of the storm to save him... from something he didn't even know was an issue.

"Okay." I nodded. "Let me see what I can do."

I grabbed my phone to call my husband. Maybe he could have the lumber delivered to us by the end of the day. Funds were still multiplying in the church account, so we could cover the extra expense. It would hold up progress, but what choice did we have?

As I was about to send the call, something clattered at the road. A pickup truck was backing into the driveway, plowing through a fresh load of gravel someone had just delivered for free.

The truck bed was full of two-by-fours, and the driver's side window was down.

I ran out to meet him. "Are these two-by-fours for us?"

"Yep." The driver, the man managing our work crew for the week, grinned. "A guy from up north somewhere called a local hardware store this morning and asked if they could donate two-by-fours to a flood victim in need."

"This is... incredible." I could hardly speak. "How many are there?"

"A hundred."

Of course there were.

By Friday, with Jerry's house mostly framed-in, we were bidding our goodbyes to our framing crew. They were a talented bunch. And throughout the entire week, as they witnessed each new miracle, they would look at each other in awe. These weren't the churchgoing, youth group volunteers. This was a professional, paid framing crew someone had donated for the week. They weren't used to all of this "God talk" on the jobsite.

We'd set up a tent at the edge of Jerry's property facing the road. There, people congregated around totes of snacks, coolers of drinks, first aid kits, muck-out suits, gloves, and other donated necessities.

Flood victims and volunteers up and down the street came to visit, stock up on supplies, and pray or share their stories.

As the day closed, we all sat under the tent, enjoying a well-deserved snack.

The contractor who had shown up the first day was also helping at another house two doors down. He walked up the road and stopped at our tent. "Courtney, I know you guys have kitchen cabinets covered here at Jerry's. Is there anyone else who would like to donate for this other house?"

In the first two weeks, we'd received (or had verbal commitments for) nearly every single item we needed to rebuild Jerry's house. I kept a notebook with names, phone numbers, and pledged materials. Watching God's master plan unfold before our eyes was remarkable. We wouldn't have to spend much of the funds still accumulating in the Save Jerry's House Fund.

"Um, I'm not sure." I went to open my phone, and just as I did, a preview message scrolled across the top of the screen.

Hi, Courtney. I'm a custom kitchen cabinetmaker...

I couldn't even speak. Tears blurred my vision, and I held out my phone for everyone in the tent to read. After he read it, one of the framing guys pulled his T-shirt up over his nose and cried.

God's fingerprints were all over everything we touched every day. I wasn't sure why He'd given us front-row seats to His handiwork, but it was the greatest show I'd ever witnessed.

And it was proof of Psalms 145:15–16: "The eyes of all look to you, and you give them their food in due season. You open your hand; you satisfy the desire of every living thing."

CHAPTER FOUR

Our workdays at Jerry's were a blur of miracles and tears seven days a week. We went from the highest highs—witnessing God's miracles—to the lowest lows, crying with devastated individuals as they struggled to reconstruct their broken lives. While I worked at Jerry's house, Paul coordinated with the other equipment operators to tear down every house with more than 50 percent damage.

We were informed these homes couldn't be repaired in their current states and would have to be built back in accordance with FEMA's new flood regulations. This meant all new rebuilds would be constructed six to eight feet in the air. Two mobile homes had washed away. Five homes were torn down completely after the fact.

One afternoon, I walked down the street to find my husband on his excavator. He was loading the last of someone's mobile home into dump trucks to be hauled away. An older gentleman stood in the road, watching. I joined him.

"That was my house," he told me, his voice shaky.

I'd never met him before. I didn't even know his name. But I put my arm around him and squeezed his shoulder. He was trembling.

"I'm so sorry," I whispered.

He clutched his chest and watched Paul work. "I haven't really followed the Lord most of my life." He sniffled, trying to regain his composure. "The truth is, my wife was always the one who went to church. She asked me to go, but I never would. I like to drink and do my own thing. I didn't want any part of it."

I kept my arm around him and let him talk.

"She had this little Jesus figurine on the mantel. It's been there for years," he went on. "When the flood first hit, we ran with our dog to the church over there, to get to higher ground. And then we stood and watched while the river took our place."

My shoulders slumped.

His face twisted up, and his gaze found mine. "When we came back to look through the debris, our stuff was just a big pile. It was a mess. We couldn't find anything. But do you know what was there on top of that pile, not broken, untouched?"

Tears filled my eyes. Because I knew what he was about to say.

"That Jesus figurine. He was right there on top. And I decided right then and there. I'm going to church with my wife. I'm turning my life around. I'm changing. Today." He sobbed as I pulled him into a hug and prayed for him.

*

By the second week of October, a mere two weeks after the flood, we stood in thankful reverence as gifts of love poured in for Jerry's house. We were already well into the second phase, rebuilding, which was unthinkable. But the victory was bittersweet because, as we looked down the road to other homes, we saw no progress. At least a dozen devastated or destroyed homes showed families who needed help. And what's more, those families were hurting, wondering why no one was coming to their aid. Why was Jerry's house getting all the attention?

One warm and sunny afternoon, we sat under Jerry's now-notorious tent with volunteers from Florida. They'd driven their church bus loaded with a dozen or so volunteers and worked every day to help flood victims. We were strangers when they arrived on Monday, but we'd become family by Friday.

One of the ladies told me about their plan to help a family on the other side of the river.

"We've kind of adopted this family and decided we're going to stay with them till they're turnkey," she explained.

Her words brought everything into focus, like God was shaking my core and opening my eyes. What a genius idea, to stay with a family until they were turnkey. To *adopt* them, in a sense.

Paul and I discussed the concept later that night. How incredible would it be if we could assess everyone's needs and find one church to adopt one family and stay with them all the way through the process—from ordering construction materials and lining up contractors to refurnishing their homes, buying clothing, and even putting gifts under the Christmas tree for their kids? What if we could make this work so every home received aid? Was it possible for us to help not just Jerry, but the entire street?

It wasn't possible for us, obviously. But I was reminded of the verse in Matthew 19:26: "But Jesus looked at them and said, 'With man this is impossible, but with God all things are possible.'"

October 11, we took a notebook and set out on foot down the street. It was a bright, warm day, and there was plenty of activity at every home.

So many church groups and ministers were working in the area. We spoke to every homeowner we could find (though some of them had left their property since their home was either uninhabitable or they were too discouraged to face the situation).

We asked each family the same questions. What were their immediate needs (vehicle, camper, food, clothing, etc.)? But then, what were the repair needs for their homes? We compiled contact numbers and information on every family member. Some of the flood survivors looked at us like we were insane. Others were aggravated by our questions, afraid to get their hopes up that someone might be stepping forward to help them. In the last two weeks, they'd already been let down by multiple government officials and insurance representatives.

After we gathered information on the present homeowners, we needed to seek out churches that could take on these projects. And where to begin?

Since the start of repairs on Jerry's house, I'd met dozens of preachers on the street. Most were passing through with volunteer crews. Others were providing food or even going door-to-door, praying with folks. My phone's contact list had grown, all new numbers from preachers of area churches. So convenient. I knew it must've been a God thing.

After all, hadn't the apostle Paul said: "And my God will supply every need of yours according to His riches in glory in Christ Jesus" (Philippians 4:19).

So I worked through the list, calling every minister or deacon or elder, matching up the homes with larger needs to the larger churches with potentially larger budgets. I approached two ministers who had been on the street since day one, Jerry Williams and Adam Stine. We'd all become friends. Each day, we exchanged God stories, prayed for one another, and discussed the progress on Clearwater Street.

We stood on the dusty street in front of Jerry's tent. Adam's jeans were covered in mud from the knees down. Pastor Jerry was handing out waters to volunteers. I beckoned both of them to join me behind the tent.

"Could you guys help me line up homes with churches?" I asked. "Can we facilitate trying to get one church to adopt one home and take care of the whole entire street? Would your churches consider taking on homes and helping with this?"

I had never met Pastor Jerry or Adam before the flood. But here we were, spending every day together. They, too, had become new members of my family circle.

"Yes, we're glad to help." Adam shook the debris dust from his cap and tucked it back on his head.

"You know that. But, Courtney, you're taking on more and more. This is too much. We need to get someone to help you organize all of this. You can't fix the whole street."

"I know." I was stubborn and delusional, sure, but I also knew God would help us.

Adam, ever the wise one with solid advice, was right when it came to my human limitations, though. I was driven and overwhelmed, running on crisis adrenaline. The choking clouds of street dust had given me laryngitis. Every night, I spent hours checking messages and organizing resources. Every day, I helped direct work crews.

I was sleep-deprived and sore all over. It was the most rewarding and most exhausting labor of love I'd ever been part of. Our own home was a mess, our businesses were suffering, and we were dragging.

But it didn't matter.

This burning eagerness to make this happen, to see this through, drove us. And the more we watched God change hearts and mend the broken and hurting, the more I was convinced. This was the most important expense of my time and energy right now. A perfect Colossians 3:2 moment: "Set your minds on things that are above, not on things that are on earth."

Pastor Jerry and Adam were anxious to get started. Their churches each adopted a home, and they reached out to more of their church leader friends as well. Pastor Jerry organized a meeting so all interested local preachers could visit the street and see the work firsthand. Two families now faced empty lots where their homes used to stand. They required full rebuilds, from the ground up. These were tall orders we were asking of these church leaders, to step out in faith and commitment to this.

Many other Clearwater Street homes needed new heat pumps, insulation and drywall, flooring, and even kitchen and bathroom remodels.

One morning, just days before the scheduled meeting, two ladies showed up at Jerry's house.

They wanted to talk to us about how they might help. One had been following my videos on the progress. The other one didn't know much about it.

She extended her hand. "Hi. I'm Beth Medders. I did some relief work as an admin some years back. Is there any way I can help you with the organizational efforts?"

I teared up and reached for my phone. "Can I have your number?"

From that day forward, Beth Medders stepped up to help us place on-the-ground volunteers and coordinate the efforts on the street. She met with churches interested in adopting or partnering to supply resources. She made spreadsheets, took photos, organized contact information, and printed handouts for every minister coming to meet with us about adopting homes. One church out of Raleigh agreed to pay Beth's salary for the next six months as our admin.

This ministry was so much bigger than us. It wasn't just one church or one denomination. It wasn't one part of the country or even one part of the world. It was every finger, toe, eye, and ear of the Lord's body coming together in unity for the common good, like the early church did.

"And all who believed were together and had all things in common. And they were selling their possessions and belongings and distributing the proceeds to all, as any had need" (Acts 2:44–45).

Days after our ministers' meeting to assess the damage on Clearwater Street, most remaining homes were adopted. Through the entire community, hundreds of volunteers from these churches arrived to sit down with homeowners and map out their game plans to put homes back together. And what's more, the volunteers cried with them, prayed with them, and compiled wish lists down to the sugar and flour in their soon-to-be-restocked pantries.

Thanks to the thousands of Facebook messages still amassing from all over the world, we were able to send our overflow resources to the other adopting churches too. If we had an extra volunteer plumber show up, we sent them to another home. If we found a surplus of donors pledging to buy kitchen appliances, we passed them down the line to the next family in need.

Our church took on another home at the end of the street for a couple named Jeff and Christine. The first day I walked into their yard, they were sitting on the front porch. A storage container was parked on what used to be their lawn. Now it was a muddy mess of broken furniture, soggy insulation, and crumbled drywall.

The couple looked overwhelmed. Defeated. Like most of their neighbors.

I introduced myself and asked what their immediate needs were.

Christine's eyes widened. "A car." She laughed.

I wrote "car" under her name. "You lost your car in the flood?" I confirmed.

"Yes. It won't start. It's sitting out there in the driveway, full of mud." She ducked her head and shuffled her feet. "I bought it brand new. And we'd just remodeled our entire kitchen last year. All new appliances and cabinets." She waved toward the direction of the kitchen, where box fans were aimed at the mud-smeared subfloor. The drywall and insulation were gone from four feet down. Their new, now-useless appliances were stacked in the garage, ready to be hauled off. Both of their garage doors were missing.

Christine told me she and Jeff had spent the first eight hours after the flood stranded on their bed with their German shepherd. "As water seeped through our floor vents, it rose quickly through the house." She gestured to the destruction and the bathroom beyond. "Then the brown floodwaters erupted through our toilets as rapids raged against the windows outside. Jeff convinced me to get up on the bed, and we sat there in horror as water levels reached the top of our mattress."

Jeff rested his hand on Christine's shoulder. "We were there for hours."

They had lost their heat pump, flooring, all insulation and drywall from four feet down, their new kitchen appliances and cabinets, and both of their bathrooms, plus their washer and dryer and two vehicles. The mud and mildew stench was overpowering. Random volunteer crews from all over had been helping with demo.

Someone from Pastor Jerry and Adam's church donated a camper for Jeff and Christine and even set it up in their backyard. Crews of college kids came in to muck out the crawl spaces. We replaced subfloor and got to work repairing their home.

That week, someone from our church donated their car for Christine. We began looking for a truck for Jeff too. One showed up for him less than two weeks later.

Christians from different denominations that used to argue over petty differences came alongside each other to serve. I attended a Christian church, but a Church of God out of LaFollette, Tennessee, partnered with us to provide appliances and supplies whenever we needed something. In the midst of the storm's aftermath, servants of Christ stepped outside their personal limitations and into the loving spirit of a collective effort.

Every night, I replied to thousands of messages from more folks wanting to help. A local man coordinated alongside another lady in town to place campers for the homeless flood survivors. Whenever someone reached out to me with a camper donation, I passed it along to him. God gathered complete strangers to work together, each with his or her own task. Over seventy campers have been donated from the time we started until now. The outpouring of generosity, watching God's family come together, was astounding.

It was more powerful and efficient than any private enterprise or government organization. And the best part was the impact it had on the homeowners and communities at large. Not only was God repairing these homes for people, He was mending their souls, easing their hurts, and drawing the volunteers closer to His peace as well. The miracles kept coming. Every day. Often multiple times a day. And we were right there in the thick of it, witnessing, our hearts full of wonder.

*

Days before Jerry's birthday, October 17, I was walking through his house, doing a video update on the progress. The HVAC guy was supposed to come today, but he couldn't because the home wasn't completely in the dry. Two doors and multiple windows still weren't installed. Our framing crew had to leave.

But wouldn't you know it? God sent us another group of highly skilled carpenters from Wisconsin, who'd been working at Jeff and Christine's house. They were eager to come set Jerry's remaining doors and windows so progress wouldn't be hindered. Another blessing.

That day, I mentioned to the Facebook followers that Jerry's seventieth birthday was three days away. I suggested that maybe we should shower him with gifts, all the items he would need to move back into his home. One of our other volunteers helped him make an extensive Amazon wish list, with everything from sheets and pillows to a shower curtain and towels, silverware, and lamps. Then we posted the link with the church address so folks could ship deliveries there. Every single item was purchased within twenty-four hours.

On his birthday, our family met Jerry for dinner at his favorite Mexican restaurant. I was so excited to give him his gift. Shortly after the flood, we found Jerry's Bible on the bridge over his creek. It was soaked in mud, and the pages were curled, the leather cover warped. I snapped a picture of it lying in the mud when we found it, a reminder of hope amidst the destruction.

"This was my most prized possession," Jerry told me that day, tears rolling down his cheeks as he tried to straighten the cover. He spent hours that afternoon painstakingly rinsing and cleaning each page as best he could. It was a Rainbow Bible. And even though he laid it in the sun to dry, the damage was beyond repair.

I handed Jerry a gift bag at his birthday dinner. Inside was a new Rainbow Bible.

Later, one of the volunteers turned my original photo of Jerry's old Bible into a black-and-white canvas to hang in his new home. The Scripture over the photo announced, "The Lord on High is mightier than the noise of many waters" (Psalm 93:4).

The day after Jerry's birthday, Lori texted me. The Amazon guy had just left our church building and unloaded his entire van into the fellowship hall. I laughed. And then, of course, I cried. Because how awesome was it that strangers from all over this earth would spend their money to send this man every needed item to get back in his home? It was surreal.

We stored all of Jerry's household goods in a commercial space we were renting until he was ready to move in. Besides the couch, recliner, coffee table, bed, and end tables, he was pretty well set.

By the third week of October, we'd passed the rough-in inspection for Jerry's house and were starting insulation. The progress was inconceivable, and I joked with my husband.

"We should race." I laughed. "With God as my project manager, I bet I can build more houses than you before Christmas."

"I don't doubt that," he said.

CHAPTER FIVE

October 20, twenty-three days after the flood, my husband stood in front of our church assembly to discuss the progress on the two homes we'd adopted and to make a plea for prayer. Our church only had about 250 members. We weren't big by any means, but because we knew God would come through, we were walking by faith to repair these homes (probably over a two-hundred-thousand-dollar commitment). We'd already watched Him do it, time and again.

After receiving quotes from several heat pump companies, we were flabbergasted. Jeff and Christine's unit was going to cost 12,200 dollars. We wanted to stretch our donations as far as possible, to be good stewards of what the Lord had provided, and we didn't know how long this work would continue.

My husband explained the situation to our church family about the lowest quote we'd received.

"Guys, we need help, so this morning, I'm asking you. Who do you know? Can you do heat pump installation? Do you know a company that could get us a better price? This is a lot of money, and we need to move forward with this quickly. Cold weather is coming."

After church, my husband and I were inundated with church members approaching, asking how they could help. A couple of folks handed me checks made out to the church. Someone gave my husband a check for the church fund as well. And our church secretary, Lori, also collected funds. Then I remembered I had another check in my purse from the Wisconsin couple who'd worked with us all week. Before we left, we handed all donations to the church secretary.

On our way home, we discussed the huge response. Paul hadn't made the announcement as a means to collect funds. He was merely asking if anyone had connections to make this heat pump possible and to request our congregation join together in prayer for the effort. Paul listed off the totals of the checks he'd received. Then I gave him the totals I'd collected, and he told me about another check given to Lori, one I didn't know about.

After we added up every check amount, I stared at the total on my phone's calculator—12,200 dollars. On the dot. I don't think we spoke for ten minutes. Our mouths hung open, and I cried.

Another God thing.

Indeed, Psalm 147:5 is true, for "Great is our Lord, and abundant in power; His understanding is beyond measure."

By the third week of October, you could walk into any given house on Clearwater Street and meet smiling people sharing food, talking about Jesus, and writing Scriptures and signing their names on the studs of open walls. New friends circled up in muddy yards to pray together. Every workday felt like a Bible study, a prayer meeting. Volunteers working on other streets in the area shared their

God stories too. It wasn't just happening on Clearwater Street. God was bringing His miracles and His spiritual revival to the entire area.

He showered hope on the hopeless and cast His light in the dark places where Satan had tried to take hold.

*

"Oh, yay! Our heat pump guys are here!" Genuinely excited, I jumped out of my car at Jeff and Christine's house on Tuesday morning, October 29. We were pushing hard to get them back in their home.

The camper they were living in was cold and tiny. Plus, it leaked. Despite the bales of straw we'd stacked underneath for extra insulation, they were miserably cold at night.

Through a local minister, we'd found an HVAC company willing to discount the system. The company spent an hour or two at Jeff and Christine's, making notes. I thanked them and asked for a timeline on the quote.

"I'm not sure." The HVAC guy tapped his pen against his clipboard. "We still have to do a quote for this one down at 732 too. Do you know who's responsible for that?"

I rubbed my temples. Somehow, with my detailed notebook of homeowners and needs, I knew nothing about 732—not even the name of who lived there. The home, a single-wide trailer, hadn't been adopted either.

"Who ordered the quote?" I lowered my hand and crossed my arms. Adam or Pastor Jerry had probably done it.

He flipped through his paperwork. "Um-hmm." His mouth turned down at the corners. "That's weird. It doesn't say."

"Well..." I opened my phone and went through our group texts. There was no info on 732. "Go ahead and do the quote, and I'll ask around to see who's paying for it."

He lowered his notes. "I'll do that."

That afternoon, I messaged the ministers and coordinators. No one claimed the HVAC quote for 732.

The lady living at 732, I later learned, was a widow. Every piece of insulation under her trailer, her ductwork, and her full heat pump system had washed away. Her home was cold. She'd powered space heaters around the clock while frigid air poured into the house through the vents she'd insulated with blankets and plastic bags.

I went to the leadership at our church.

"Could we cover the heat pump cost for this other lady?" I asked, despite it being a big obligation. After all, we'd committed to rebuilding two homes before we had the money in the account to do it. Then again, this wasn't our money or even our plan. Every time we stepped out in faith, God matched us step for step.

"Sounds like God's already ordered it." One of the men shrugged.

My heart swelled and my eyes filled. This group of brothers and sisters showed their steel faith.

One week later, the HVAC man was back at Jeff and Christine's.

"Hey, I meant to tell you!" I stopped him before he left. "Our church is going to cover the heat pump for 732, so you can go ahead and get started on it."

The guy furrowed his eyebrows. "I know. It's in my notes. That's where I'm headed next, to start working on its install."

I tilted my head to one side. "Someone's already taking care of that heat pump? Who ordered it?"

Again, he flipped through his clipboard pages. "Uh, I don't know. There's not a name. There's just an order to install it."

I could only shake my head. "Well, when you're done, make sure you send the bill for this one and 732 both to Central Community Christian Church. Thank you."

Weeks went by, and I heard nothing from the HVAC company. Lori asked when they were going to bill the church, so I called the company and explained the situation.

"What's the address again?" the office lady asked. "I don't see it here."

"It's 732. Our church is supposed to pay the balance for that house." I explained we were responsible for the bill on Jeff and Christine's house as well.

"Can I put you on hold?"

She went away for what seemed like an eternity. I wondered if we'd gotten cut off. When she came back on the phone, her tone had warmed. "The balance for both of those homes is zero dollars."

I couldn't speak for the clench in my chest. I swallowed hard. Then my voice cracked. "Who paid it? Did someone else pay it?"

"All I know is the balance is zero dollars," she said.

After we got off the phone, I must have cried for half an hour, calling every person in our group to relay the story. God had ordered, installed, and covered the heat pump installation for a flood victim we'd overlooked... a widow lady who truly needed it. Not to mention the heat pump for Jeff and Christine. These miracles were just another reminder. The recovery work wasn't our project. It was God's. And as long as He was in the driver's seat, He would mend every broken piece in His time.

One week later, we were on Clearwater Street meeting a drywall guy from Texas. It was late, after dark. A young man walked by, and we introduced ourselves. He was the widow's grandson, Billy, and he was beyond grateful they finally had working heat in their home.

"How are you guys? Do you need anything?" my husband asked.

"No, sir. We can't thank you enough for all you've done," Billy said.

"It wasn't us. It was God," my husband clarified. "Is there anything else, at all, you need right now?"

Billy shook his head no, then hesitated. "I have everything I need, except my chickens. I sure do miss my chickens. They washed away in the flood. But I don't need any more. We're so blessed. We don't need anything."

Three days later, I was very behind on my Facebook messages. (I confess I stayed behind throughout the duration of the relief work.) It was close to bedtime, but I was trying to reply to as many folks as I could before turning in for the night.

I clicked on a message from a lady in California. I burst into giggles. I received peculiar messages sometimes with folks wanting to donate all sorts of stuff. Sometimes the messages were funny, and sometimes I read them to my husband. Most of the time, they were exactly what we needed.

"What?" He sat next to me.

"Listen to this one." I tipped my phone screen toward him. "This lady from California says, 'Hey, I know this is random. But I actually have some fertilized chicken eggs I'd be willing to ship'—" I stopped talking and threw my hand over my mouth, because I remembered Billy. And then my happy tears fell. She wanted to send fertilized chicken eggs. And Billy needed chickens. "Paul, the time stamp shows it was sent Sunday night about midnight... just hours after our conversation with Billy."

*

God's miracles tumbled from the sky every day. If we needed a specific tool, it appeared on a jobsite. If one house had leftover insulation, another house needed exactly that amount. If we ran out of drywall, someone, even from another state, pulled up with a trailer full of drywall.

It became almost comical. God provided so much, so often, that we stood and laughed, even as the tears streamed down, shaking our heads at it all. It didn't matter how many times He came through for us; it was no less inspiring and miraculous the two hundred and fiftieth time than it was the first time. He was just shining, showing us how much He loved and cared for every detail of this work.

The more we magnified His name and told His stories on social media, the more the ministry grew. People were hungry for the God stories. They loved hearing about our Father coming through for His children.

And we never asked for donations. I didn't even post the church link unless someone requested it. I merely told about the loving favors God provided every day.

Hearts were touched from the volunteers who drove in from Arkansas, California, Colorado, Florida, Georgia, Iowa, Kansas, Kentucky, Maryland, Mississippi, New York, North and South Carolina, Ohio, Oklahoma, Pennsylvania, Texas, Virginia, Washington, and Wisconsin. But hearts were also touched for the flood victims and the people giving and participating through social media. It was God's master plan.

CHAPTER SIX

Good thing God was our lead coordinator. The collection of resources was too much for one person or even one church to track. But God, in His wisdom, sent us the right churches to adopt the right homes and distribute the workload. Volunteers from Poplar Ridge Christian Church worked regularly on Clearwater Street at the home they'd adopted, Jeff Fuller's house, one of the hardest hit. Their house was two doors down from Jeff and Christine's, and he and his daughter had ridden out the storm inside, where the floodwaters rose four feet.

Like many of the other damaged homes, his needed a new kitchen and remodeled bathrooms, all appliances, including a heat pump, plus flooring and siding and every piece of furniture—not to mention personal belongings. Once the floodwaters receded and the demo was complete, his home was a vacant shell.

From the first day postflood, Jeff got right to work repairing his house. But the day I met him, maybe a week after Hurricane Helene came through, he was sitting in his front porch swing, eyes teary and shoulders slumped. Devastated that their beautiful home had been destroyed, he admitted he felt helpless.

That same week, Brad and Shawna Perry called me. Brad was the minister of Poplar Ridge Christian Church I'd attended several years before. They both wanted to discuss the possibility of adopting a bigger project on the street. Their church family was a body of believers intent on service, so they'd be a wonderful fit to shine God's light on this hurting community.

The day they committed to Jeff Fuller's house, Poplar Ridge jumped right in. They were relentless and efficient. Sometimes, as many as twenty volunteers from their church were working at Jeff's house. Coming through the front door for a visit, I was met with music, and laughter echoed along the walls. Jeff knew every volunteer's name, and he'd started attending the worship services at their church too.

"Look at this progress! You guys are awesome!" I spun around to take in the full scope of it.

Brad smiled. "You wanna race and see if we can get Jeff Fuller back in his house before you guys get Jeff and Christine back in theirs?"

I laughed.

Jeff chimed in. "I'm not going to be back in by Christmas. I'm moving back in by Thanksgiving!"

"I believe it." I rocked back on my heels, breathing in the smell of drywall mud and sawdust. It was October. Yet they'd completed the drywall and were about to begin painting. They'd even ordered flooring.

I wandered out front. Vehicles were parked in the dried river silt all over Jeff's yard. They lined the street too. Two doors down, more vehicles had parked at Jeff and Christine's—workers coming in and out of the house carrying supplies.

Someone walked up behind me, so I turned.

Jeff Fuller stopped a few feet away. A wide grin stretched across his face, and his eyes gleamed.

"You know"—he waved toward the work in progress—"when all of this first happened, I thought it was the worst possible thing. I didn't know what I was going to do. But now, today, I can say I believe more good has come from this disaster than evil. I've watched God do big things." Then he hugged me, and we both cried.

How true David's words were in Psalm 9:9–10: "The Lord is a stronghold for the oppressed, a stronghold in times of trouble. And those who know Your name put their trust in You, for You, O Lord, have not forsaken those who seek You."

Brad joined us then. "Hey, before I forget, one of our church members has a nearly new stainless steel refrigerator. If you hear of someone who needs it, let me know."

"Okay."

I thanked him and jotted down the information in my notebook, unsure of where God would use this item in His time. He always had a plan.

Then one frigid morning in late October, we had a new need. I'd stopped in at Jeff and Christine's. Jeff was crouched on his living room floor. Half of the subfloor was missing, and the mud underneath was exposed. The room smelled musty, and he looked tired—and understandably so, since he and his wife were still sleeping in that tiny camper in the backyard with their big German shepherd.

"Miss Courtney, do you know anyone who has kerosene?" he asked.

This was a common problem in the disaster zones. Kerosene prices were sky high. Some flood victims spent as much as fifty dollars a day just to heat their homes while the work was being done. We were still drying out floors to kill mold too, so heat was essential.

"I'm not sure." I twisted my mouth to one side. "I don't have access to kerosene right now, but we'll pray about it and work on it. I'll let you know if I hear something."

I walked away from his house and back down the street, kicking at the mounds of dried mud on the broken asphalt as if I could remove the stumbling blocks from our paths. Jeff looked so discouraged. I wanted to help, but we couldn't supply kerosene for everyone. We would put a serious dent in our rebuilding funds. There were just too many needs.

Hours later, as the sun rose higher and it started warming up a little, a group of us sat under the tent in front of Jerry's house. We rehydrated and reviewed the construction plans. We had tons of volunteers that day, college students helping muck out crawl spaces and others coming in for demolition. Jerry's home was in the dry now, wrapped and ready for siding. As we discussed the next steps, a long line of trucks rolled onto the street with Kentucky tags. Some of the vehicles were hauling side-by-sides and ATVs on trailers. The first truck stopped in front of Jerry's property and lowered their window.

"You guys need some kerosene down here?" the passenger asked.

I swallowed. "Yes. Desperately."

"Well, good." Beaming, he motioned to the

truck bed with his thumb. "'Cause we have about fifty jugs. And kerosene heaters. Where should we take them?"

"Everywhere." I waved toward the rest of the block. "The whole street."

The Kentucky crew piled out of their trucks and began unloading supplies onto the side-by-sides to be delivered to multiple homes.

"How did you know to come here?" I asked a guy in a blue Kentucky hat.

He stopped unloading and smiled. "When we heard about your area, our church began praying about how we could help. We decided it would be best if we could buy up a bunch of kerosene and heaters and bring them down here to deliver. We raised a good bit of money for the project. So here we are."

I couldn't believe it. I mean, I could. Obviously. I'd been watching God's miracles every day. But this team, who'd been planning for weeks, came the day we needed them. And they'd never contacted us to let us know they were coming or asked where they should bring the delivery or on what day.

These faith-filled brothers not only delivered kerosene that afternoon. They also prayed with flood survivors and spoke to people about Jesus. They stayed for hours, asking for details on the needs. Who still hadn't been adopted? What building supplies were we missing?

I met their minister, Michael Marcum, and a deacon from their church, Jamie Burkett.

"We have two complete rebuilds no one has adopted yet." I cleaned the grime off my sunglasses with my T-shirt sleeve. "We keep asking some of the bigger churches in our area. But so far, no one wants to take them on. The commitment is too big— at least a hundred and fifty grand needed for each home."

One family's house had just been torn down. Then another family, consisting of an elderly man in a wheelchair and his granddaughter, had witnessed their double-wide trailer wash away. The first family was staying in a rented apartment. The elderly man and his granddaughter were staying with family up the road in a single-wide trailer with no heat.

Five days later, Michael called me.

"Courtney, we met with the men from our church this morning, and we've committed to building those two homes for the families there."

I couldn't even talk. I was sobbing, praising God.

"That's incredible!" I finally said. "This is huge! How many members do you have in your church?"

"Oh, I don't know. About a hundred and fifty?"

I nodded, unable to speak again. I couldn't help but think about Moses and David. Joseph. Peter. Paul. I thought about the disciples, whom our Savior chose. A tiny group.

God wasn't orchestrating His miracles here on Clearwater Street from Goliaths or mighty nations. He appeared to us in a whisper, using the little folks in the shadows, the broken, those few in number. The smaller churches. He didn't need *us* to fulfill His will. And there I was, soliciting great big churches all along, forgetting God was the one at the helm. He was steering.

When we got off the phone, I was granted the privilege of calling each family to tell them what the

Lord had done. The elderly man's granddaughter had to step outside. I'd called her at work. She was wailing and crying, so ecstatic. She just couldn't believe it.

"Why are they doing this for us? Thank you! Why is everyone helping?"

I wiped under my eyes as I paced through the dirt in Jerry's front yard. "It's just a God thing."

After the call, I thanked God for the opportunity, once again, to be part of something so much bigger than me. It was God who listened to our every prayer and provided His hurting children with the seemingly impossible.

We merely stood and watched Him work.

CHAPTER SEVEN

At 8:00 a.m., I'd just finished cleaning up the breakfast dishes. I was wiping down our countertops when my phone showed an incoming call out of Atlanta, Georgia.

"Hi, Courtney. My name is Alan, and I work with a large commercial drywaller in the southeastern United States. We'd love to come and do the insulation and drywall on Jerry's house," the man on the other end told me. He'd sent a message to the inbox of my Facebook page weeks before, and I'd made a note of the donation. But I was still sorting through messages for hours each night, taking notes on who wanted to supply which item. When God opened the floodgates of building materials and work crews, the current was strong.

I tried to refrain from jumping up and down,

but I couldn't stop an escaping squeal. "That is so wonderful! We can't thank you enough!"

Alan was just one of the many volunteers God sent us right on time. God had supplied an electrician who went to church with Jerry. He'd also sent two local volunteers who reframed interior walls, once Jerry's house was in the dry. God sent a nineteen-year-old skilled carpenter from Colorado who stayed and worked with us for two weeks and did odds and ends, from plumbing to electrical work to putting in mailboxes for those who'd lost theirs in the flood.

Jerry's flooring was already picked out and on its way from California. A man in Virginia had called about doing the kitchen cabinets and granite countertops for both Jerry's house and Jeff and Christine's house. Another man from Jerry's church volunteered his entire professional paint crew. The lady from Maryland, donating bathroom vanities for both homes, sent me her website so the homeowners could select their preferred styles.

Men from West Virginia came to hang drywall in Jeff and Christine's house. Two churches had worked together to finish the insulation on their house the week before. A local Christian named Scott, who worked frequently up and down the street, checked in to fill the gaps where we'd missed things.

Every single time we uncovered a new need, we merely had to speak it, and God delivered. If we didn't see the need being met, sometimes God dropped it right in front of our faces, while we were still working to remedy the problem on our own.

Late one night, while checking messages, I received a text from a lady who said her husband was a carpenter and she wanted to come help as well. But she was homeschooling her kids. She would be bringing them along too.

I was exhausted and admittedly grouchy. We'd been working on Jerry's street almost every single day for six weeks straight. My house was a disaster, I was behind on laundry, and I hadn't cooked dinner but once or twice since the work started. I loved the blessing of being part of this tremendous endeavor, but I was acting human. And fatigued.

"I don't have anything for these people to do," I told Paul that night. "They want to come in and spend the week. We're at a standstill until the drywall sanding is done at Jeff and Christine's. And we don't have the insulation or drywall done at Jerry's either. There may be a couple of little framing things her husband could do at Jerry's. But I'm out of ideas, and I'm tired of finding jobs for people."

Like I said, I was grouchy. I'd grown weary in well-doing and made it about me.

I should have considered Galatians 6:9: "And let us not grow weary of doing good, for in due season we will reap, if we do not give up."

Paul shrugged. He was remarkably supportive of the work, patient with me as I was constantly checking messages and making notes and taking calls. But he'd gone back to work in our businesses while I kept doing relief work. He was the breadwinner.

"I don't know, Courtney. Maybe God has a plan you don't know about," he said.

I'm ashamed to admit it, but inside I rolled my eyes at him... because I didn't think he knew what he was talking about. And did I mention I was grouchy?

I replied to the lady and told her I didn't have much for her or her kids to do, but they could come if they wanted and maybe help out at the local food bank in town.

The day before they arrived, the drywall job at Jeff and Christine's was completed. It was time for a paint day, and I made a video to be shown at our church, hoping to encourage folks to come out and help. So far, I was the only scheduled painter on the entire house.

Every day, I bounced back and forth between Jerry's house and Jeff and Christine's, trying to manage work crews and order supplies. The man who'd volunteered to build Jerry's back deck bailed on us the week before, and I couldn't find anyone to take his place. Maybe I was also grouchy because my tennis elbow was getting bad. Carpal tunnel was too. There wasn't much time for self-care or even sleep. We'd taken on more than we could manage.

Obviously, I was still making it about me instead of leaning on God's strong arms.

The day the volunteer family arrived, Jennifer and her husband, Travis, met me at Jerry's house. I took them inside to show them around so Travis could see the few framing issues we needed fixed.

"That's really all I have for you to do right now," I explained. "You'll probably have this knocked out within a couple of hours."

He motioned out the French doors into the backyard. "What's with the deck?"

"Oh. That." I sighed. "The guy who committed to building the deck never finished. He just put the posts in."

"So you need the deck built?" Travis asked.

I released the breath I'd been holding. "Can you... do that?"

Travis grinned. "It's what I do for a living. I build decks."

Tears stung my eyes. Of course he did.

"Well, thank you," I said, still flabbergasted. "If you need me, I'll be down the street at Jeff and Christine's. We're having a paint day, but no volunteers have shown up." And it was a holiday, so my nine-year-old daughter was out of school, tagging along with me, grumbling all the way.

"You need help painting?" Jennifer piped up. She was standing in the corner with her two girls, ages eight and six.

"Um, yeah," I said. "Actually, I would love some help painting."

"I always end up painting when we work on a house," she explained. "It's kind of my thing."

Right. Of course it was.

"And since you have your daughter, maybe our girls could play together while we work," she suggested.

The clichéd lightbulb went off in my head, and I thought back to my husband's words. Yes, God had a plan. Much bigger than mine. If I could have just gotten out of my way and followed His lead, this work would have been so much easier. I asked God, once again, to forgive me.

Over the next three days, Jennifer and I painted that entire house together. Our girls became the best of friends, playing outside in the dirt and sharing toys and giggling like they'd always known each other. Meanwhile, we shared our personal testimonies of faith with each other and talked about God's interventions in our lives, sometimes stopping what we were doing so we could cry and hug each other. She became one of my favorite volunteers.

The day she left, I cried and told her I loved her. I was so thankful God had sent her family to supply every demand at the exact time we needed them. I don't know what we would have done otherwise.

That afternoon, I received a text from an elder at our church. He needed a refrigerator and flooring for another flood victim in the Valley Forge area, someone named Randy. Since Brad had told me about the member of the Poplar Ridge Christian Church who had a stainless steel refrigerator, I sent him her contact so they could meet up. God had sent us that resource weeks before we needed it. Just like He'd sent Jennifer and Travis.

The next week, the man from Lafollette Church of God rounded up appliances in Knoxville to deliver to Jeff and Christine's. He found not only kitchen appliances but also a washer and dryer. And when those were installed, God sent us more wonderful, highly skilled volunteers from out West. This was their third trip to come and help. They finished trimming Jeff and Christine's entire house, and we had them over for dinner. We loved these people like family.

Every Tuesday morning, I met with Pastor Jerry, Adam, and Beth to discuss the various projects on the street. We kept tabs on the other churches that had adopted homes to see how they were coming along, and we dispersed volunteer crews where needed and shared resources. We were able to help quite a few of the homes with "lesser damage" that had slipped between the cracks. Sometimes it was a matter of mucking out crawl spaces and reinsulating under a trailer. Other times it was providing underpinning or graveling their driveway.

Each meeting though, we spent the majority of our time laughing and crying, sharing our God stories of the week. And I want to add—it wasn't just happening to our group. It was happening on jobsites over the entire area. Every adopting church was supplied with its needs. Our Kentucky friends had raised three hundred thousand in a matter of *weeks*. Another couple working on River Road in the Valley Forge area, Curtis and Desie Gentry, had taken on nine homes, single-handedly. God was giving them lumber and appliances and workers too.

Our faith was renewed daily.

CHAPTER EIGHT

As we sailed through November, we saw more than physical homes being restored. We also witnessed the pouring of eternal foundations. And we finally realized God's entire plan was focused on revival, not rebuilding.

I had my "Author Courtney Dailey" page on Facebook, but I'd been struggling for years to get a book published. Every morning during prayer time, for a full two years before Hurricane Helene, I would say to the Lord, "Please help me be a bright light and have massive impact for You." I would repeat that statement over and over, with the implication that God would give me a book deal and I could become a *New York Times* bestselling author and impact lives. Obviously. Because it was all about *my* plan, and I was just hoping God would bless it.

Then one night, just before bed, I read a message from a lady in Ohio. She was depressed and struggling with her faith. She wanted to believe, but she'd endured a great deal of church hurt in her past. We ended up talking on the phone for forty-five minutes about Jesus, crying and sharing our personal stories. When I got off the phone, I climbed out of bed (makeup still running down my face) and went to my office so I could make a video for my Facebook friends.

It had finally dawned on me. God was answering that prayer I'd muttered on my knees every day for the last couple of years. At last, I was fulfilling what I'd set out to do: shining His light to a worldwide audience and having massive impact... sans the dreamy book deal.

My Facebook inbox was jam-packed with personal conversations. Bible studies.

One person wrote to me and confessed he struggled with gender identity. Someone else's son was sentenced to prison for murder. Another individual had just received the news that their cancer was back. One lady's husband was in a plane crash. And on and on, it went.

Most of the dear souls writing to me would never have walked into a bookstore, picked up one of my Christian fiction books, and reached out to me for prayer or Bible study. But because of Hurricane Helene and the unique situation we found ourselves in, I was able to connect with a different audience. I could meet people on a personal level. I made hundreds of friends, prayed with them, cried with them... But most importantly, I shared God's love with them. We welcomed strangers into our home, cooked for them, and loved on them.

This spiritual awakening wasn't limited to my Facebook followers either. It was happening all around us, in other ways. Especially on jobsites.

We had a volunteer named Gabe who drove twelve hours to come work with us. He didn't believe in God. But he was a carpenter, and he had a heart to serve. So he drove in with his tools, not knowing what God had in store for him. On Gabe's first day on the jobsite, he joined up with one of our work crews from a church out of Mississippi. These were God-fearing, testifying men.

Gabe wasn't there five minutes before he started using foul language. An elderly gentleman on the crew, the lead volunteer on the project, stopped the work and asked everyone to circle up.

"Before we begin our workday," the man announced, "let's all bow our heads together and pray."

Then he led us in the most beautiful, convicting prayer—admonishing God as our Savior, thanking Him for our salvation. It was a prayer of praise and thanksgiving. Several in the circle were crying by the time he said amen.

We never heard Gabe use another curse word on the jobsite after that. As a matter of fact, upon Gabe's return home, he called that same elderly gentleman to ask him about becoming a follower of Jesus. Gabe was impacted by the positive Christian influences he'd witnessed. They discussed planning another work trip so they could baptize Gabe in the very river that brought them together.

Prayers on the jobsite were a regular occurrence, as were Bible studies. Many of the volunteers signed the two-by-fours of the flooded homes with their names, Scriptures, and where they'd traveled from.

One day, a lady walked up to Jerry's tent and said, "Would you like a Bible?"

Dozens of people walked up and down the street every day. Some were moms with young children who felt a God nudge to bring snacks to workers. Others delivered full meals and set up tables to serve. Some came from churches to distribute collected supplies. It got to be so much, my husband brought down his enclosed trailer to store the surplus.

Jerry's tent was our hub for first aid, masks, muck-out suits and work gloves, tools, snacks, waters, and a host of other things.

"Ma'am, I have a Bible. Thank you, though. Give that to someone else who needs it," Jerry told her.

"Well, you have plenty of supplies here. Let me

just give you this. You never know when someone will need it," she insisted.

So Jerry took the Bible, put it on the table behind him, and thanked her.

Ten minutes later, a truck arrived from the Red Cross. Three volunteers approached Jerry's tent, clipboards in hand.

"Can we help you with anything?" they asked Jerry.

"I have everything I need." He pointed to the sign hanging on the tent, a decorative piece of artwork that previously hung in his house. There was just one word, in big, bold letters: *Blessed*. Jerry had a volunteer zip-tie the framed piece to the front of his tent the week after the flood.

"What does that mean?" the lady asked.

"God has given me everything I need. You wouldn't believe it if I told you. He's sent people and construction materials to rebuild my house."

The lady frowned. "Hmm. A lot of people down here talk about God. I don't know much about Him, to be honest. I don't even own a Bible."

Jerry raised his eyebrows and smiled, turning

around to grab the Bible behind him. He handed it to the lady. "Here. I think this is for you."

The Red Cross didn't give Jerry anything that day or in the days to follow. He did have everything he needed. But he gave that one volunteer what she needed most.

Samuel, another flood victim on the street, was studying the Bible with the men rebuilding his house. He hadn't been to church in years, but he'd gone through some difficult things in his life.

"He used to be active in church," the minister told me. "He even drove the church bus and taught Sunday school."

"What happened?" I asked.

"You know how it is. He just lost his way. But the Lord is working on him. I can see it."

"That's wonderful. Keep studying with him. Keep encouraging him," I said.

One month later, the minister called me. "I have to tell you this story!"

"Yeah?"

"Yeah. So Sunday, I was in the sound room at church, and they kept asking me questions and stalling me. You know how Sundays are. It's stressful, and I had to preach. It was almost time to start. But I felt like these guys were making me late on purpose. When I finally got to the sanctuary, guess who was in the choir box, holding a hymnal, singing?"

"Who?"

"Samuel!"

I squeezed my eyes tight as something deep inside me shifted. "No way!"

"Yes! And he brought his girlfriend too!"

"Praise God."

God was working on so many hearts up and down that street. One other flood survivor, Ralph, was feeling the effects of God's tugs on his heart. I was standing in Jerry's front yard one day when Ralph stopped his Bronco and put down the window.

"Can I talk to you a minute?" he called out to me.

I went to his truck window. "Sure. What's up?"

He flicked ash off his lit cigarette. Hurt and discouragement lined his face, not unlike many others on this street. Then the tears began to fall. He sniffed. "I've been trying to help people."

"I know." I laid my hand on the windowsill. "I've been watching you working like crazy. You're collecting supplies and delivering them to folks and helping people who aren't in their homes. Even though there's tons of work to do on your own house, you're focused on others."

"It's strange." His voice was thick. "I know this sounds crazy, but I feel like the Lord has been chasing me for forty days."

I bowed my head in quiet agreement, because I understood. God had left the ninety-nine to come looking for me, once upon a time. Ralph was feeling the powerful effects of His Father's love, with open arms, waiting for His prodigal to come home. Squeezing his heart.

That's what God's love did. He didn't love us conditionally or give up on us when we fell down. He didn't get angry when we questioned or grew sad or depressed or we didn't understand. God waited for us, longing to gather us in His arms and make things right. He wanted to give us an eternity of nothing but joy.

God was showing all of us... from the workers to the unbelieving volunteers to the flood victims to the corporate and government organizations. He was radiating the power of His love and peace. He revealed who was really in charge, at the control panel. And it wasn't us. Every day, He reminded us we were happiest when we rested in His grace—secure, safe, in Him.

He demonstrated nothing but unending love. And our thirsty souls drank it willingly.

CHAPTER NINE

Thanksgiving was just around the corner. God had powered us through exactly two months of relief work, and Jerry's home was nearly complete. Jeff and Christine's home wasn't far behind, still neck and neck with Jeff Fuller's house.

Beth was busy organizing a massive Thanksgiving dinner for families on the street with nowhere to go. Our church was hosting a Thanksgiving dinner too. Temperatures loomed in the thirties, and the leaves were long gone from every tree. But that didn't deter the stream of volunteers still surging into our community.

One night, a Texas man called to discuss meeting me and other relief workers in the community to help us get organized. Someone had shared my videos with him. He invited me to lunch and asked if I could bring the coordinators from the Valley Forge area too.

He was talking about Curtis and Desie Gentry, the couple who had taken on nine homes across the river. They'd been working six or seven days a week for the last two months. I texted and told Desie about the meeting. She and her husband were overwhelmed, so taking the time to meet with us was a big deal for her.

The lunch didn't work out as we'd hoped. It turned out, the folks wanting to help us were a better fit for a different area. But after lunch, as Desie and I visited in the parking lot, she filled me in on the work progress in their area. They were rebuilding a mile or two up the road from us. We were both so busy, running in different directions, we never would have made the time to talk—if it hadn't been for that lunch meeting. I was convinced it was a divine appointment. God wanted us to talk that day.

See, I had no idea Curtis and Desie were actually working on twenty-four homes, not nine. Twelve of the families were completely displaced.

Some stayed in cold campers or with nearby family. We had tremendous resources via the Facebook volunteers. Curtis and Desie didn't have that kind of help. No crews had even come in with heavy machinery to remove debris. No homes had been adopted by churches.

Many of the adopted folks on our street were scheduled to be back in their homes by Thanksgiving or right around Christmas. And, to be honest, I was getting excited about the countdown for the two homes we were managing. My husband and I were dragging, though we were so grateful to be a part of the work. We didn't feel worthy to witness the things we watched God do every day. But if we could just get Jerry and Jeff and Christine in their homes by Thanksgiving, we could get back to living our lives. Back to normal.

After my conversation with Desie, I realized that wasn't happening. Not even close. There were still so many needs, so much to be done in our area. And there were still churches out there willing to donate and adopt families. So we started trying to connect these churches to Curtis and Desie, to help them.

I called Paul after I left the restaurant, a new tug in my heart. "Honey, we might need to have Curtis and Desie over for dinner soon," I told him. "They are absolutely drowning over there, working themselves to death. We have to see how we can help them."

"So you're saying we won't be finished by Christmas, after all?" he asked.

We both laughed because we already knew this, somewhere deep down.

The flood-relief fund at church grew every day. We were wondering why God kept sending materials. Obviously, He wasn't done yet. And this wasn't our project or even our church's project. It was the Lord's project.

That night, on my way home from my daughter's gymnastics class, I got a call from an unknown number. And because of the nature of the work, I answered every call.

"Is this Courtney Dailey?" the lady on the phone asked.

"Yes, ma'am."

"Oh, thank goodness! It's taken me forever to get your number! I'm sorry to bother you. I really need you."

"Okay?"

"Can you come up with a reason to get Jerry to this car dealership in Johnson City tomorrow at eleven a.m.? Someone is buying him a car, and they want it to be a surprise!"

"Are you serious?"

"Yes! Isn't it wonderful? A local man has been raising funds to provide vehicles in the area to flood victims."

My throat went dry. "That is unreal."

"I know! So if you can please come up with some reason to get Jerry there in the morning, that's all I need."

"Okay. Thank you so much!"

After the call, I went home and brainstormed with my husband. I was giddy. Since Jerry needed to start shopping for furniture soon, we had the perfect excuse.

The next morning, I told Jerry I was coming to pick him up and we were heading to Johnson City to shop for furniture. The church had given us a budget, and Jerry was snowed under with the prospect of selecting everything he needed. The list was extensive—from love seats and a coffee table to a bed and kitchen table and lamps and rugs. Plus, he wouldn't let me forget his dream recliner. We shopped for an hour or two, and then Paul called.

"I'm over here at the dealership, and I need a ride. Can you come get me?" he asked.

We'd worked out the whole scheme. I was there fifteen minutes later and turned off the engine.

Jerry waved me on. "I'll just stay in the car."

"No, get out with me." I panicked. "I want to show you a car in the showroom."

He snorted and crossed his arms. "No thanks."

I laughed. "Jerry, just get out of the car and come with me!"

He was not happy about my insistence, but he followed me into the showroom. Once we walked in, Jerry craned around. "Where's Paul?"

"Hmm. I don't know."

A man approached, glowing, a wide smile on his face. He held out his hand, and Jerry shook it.

"Mr. Poole! How are you, sir?" His voice boomed.

Jerry's eyebrows knit together. "Fine, thank you." He gave me a side-glance.

The man shook my hand too. "Why don't you two have a seat over there in the waiting area, and we'll be with you in a moment?"

"Okay. Thank you," I said.

Jerry followed me to the sitting area. "Where's Paul?"

I shrugged and ran my finger along my phone screen, afraid my face would betray the surprise.

We sat, and Jerry turned to me. "Courtney, who was that man?"

"I have no idea." I couldn't look at him.

"Yeah, but he knew my name. I've never seen him before in my life."

"Are you sure? You know the whole world."

"No." He shook his head. "Uh-uh. Not him."

"I don't know. That's weird."

"Where's Paul?" He bounced his knee and tapped his thumb against the armrest.

"Uh, let me text him." I typed into my phone. Just how long could I keep up the charade?

A different man approached us then and stuck out his hand. "Hi, Jerry. My name's Hanes Torbett."

I switched my phone to video mode and hit the red record button.

"Are you ready to get started?" Hanes asked.

"Get started with what?" Jerry blinked, all deer in the headlights.

"To sign the papers for your car."

"My what—?" Jerry's gaze darted back and forth between the two of us.

"He doesn't know," I whispered to Hanes.

"Oh. He doesn't know." He turned to Jerry. "You're getting a car today, brother."

Jerry's head swiveled back and forth again, and the color drained from his face. "I can't afford no car."

"You don't have to pay for it, Jerry. It's covered," I told him.

"Come on out front!" Hanes slapped his hands together. "I'll show you!"

I followed Hanes and a bewildered Jerry to the front lot. A midsized, shiny black SUV was parked there. It wasn't brand new, but it was very nice. Speechless, Jerry went around to the back of the car and hid his face and cried.

Hanes had been on a quest to help flood victims since the end of September. But his calling was different from ours. First, it began with fuel for people in the mountains, to keep their generators running. He, too, had experienced multiple God moments... provisions that could only come from the Lord.

He couldn't wait to tell me his story.

"Right after the hurricane hit, I put a post out on Facebook, telling folks where I was going and what I was doing that day. So many people needed fuel. I didn't know how much I could raise, but I posted my Venmo link. Then I went to Walmart and bought cans and started filling up. I checked my Venmo while I was there, but no one had donated. It didn't matter. I was doing this either way. My total at the checkout was seven hundred and eighty-nine dollars. When I got in my car and opened my Venmo again, there was eight hundred in the account."

After the fuel runs, Hanes raised money to buy vehicles for folks. Over the next few months, he raised enough to buy twelve cars for people who'd lost everything. Jerry just happened to be one of the people on his list.

CHAPTER TEN

By November 15, the flooring was going in at Jerry's, and the crew from Kentucky had come in to do finish work, nailing down trim. The kitchen cabinet guy arrived from Virginia, installing cabinets and countertops at both houses. I won't pretend the relief work was all marshmallows and rainbows throughout the duration. Just like every Bible story, the working parts of God's masterpiece were comprised of humans. And we were all flawed. And tired. And cranky. Add to that the PTSD of flood survivors and the highly emotional state of crisis we'd been wading through for two whole months.

Jerry was a family friend for about fifteen years before the flood, but he always called me his adopted daughter. He was stubborn, and I was too.

When we disagreed about something, there were fireworks.

He insisted he wanted his beautiful, donated-from-California flooring installed on a diagonal. I insisted that putting down the flooring like that would be much more complicated, use more material, and be totally outdated. He persisted. I argued. And he finally told me it was his house and he needed to make some decisions on his own without my input.

I so wanted to get him in his house by Thanksgiving so badly. I was pushing. Hard. It was cold, and we were exhausted. In my efforts to get things done, I was railroading him, trying to propel us to the finish line. And he didn't appreciate my assertiveness.

We didn't speak for two days. And though we both finally apologized, the tension remained for weeks. In that time, our progress on Clearwater Street ground to a halt. There were delays on every project. Jerry's new car broke down. We couldn't get his HVAC guy to finish the job. When the man came in to install his kitchen cabinets, a piece of granite fell and smashed one cabinet door. The kitchen cabinet order for Jeff and Christine was incorrect. The plumbing for their kitchen sink was improperly completed. The mattress we ordered for them was damaged. Their HVAC system wasn't working properly. And their donated truck broke down too.

I came home every evening for a solid week on the brink of tears, not standing in awe of God's miracles and leaning on Him, but hunched over, defeated and wiped out, relying on myself. Complaining. Tired. I didn't have the energy to keep managing the homes or even to check my messages. I wanted to quit. Just be done. And my attitude reflected my contrary heart.

Our retail business was suffering, and I was missing out on valuable time with my family. I'd thrown myself so hard into the work, day and night, that I'd lost my balance. It was a feeling of defeat. My husband had gone back to work, building homes for our other business. I missed him. There was too much sleep-deprivation and overcommitment. It was my greatest flaw, time and again, thinking it was up to *me*, trying to do things *myself,* instead of relying on God's plan.

One night, after a frustrating day, I was reading through Facebook messages. The inbox was about three weeks behind, and the task of replying was daunting. Then I opened a message from a lady in Georgia. She said she just had to let me know what she and her husband had done.

They'd been following the videos and the work since the beginning. They decided to copy our model and travel to Burnsville, North Carolina, where they had adopted three families. Their goal was to rebuild the homes and stay with these flood survivors until they were turnkey, providing every need—even furniture—until the task was complete.

I dropped my chin to my chest and sobbed, repenting for my bad attitude. This work, this area-wide explosion of revival and love and community, had nothing to do with me. God's plan was perfect, and He was in control. I had to stop trying to run everything. And I had to stop, in general, to find rest in Him and lay my worries at the foot of the cross.

At our next Tuesday meeting, I confessed to Pastor Jerry, Adam, and Beth about my bad attitude. I told them how poorly everything had gone on our two projects and asked for their prayers.

I cried. "Our Wisconsin crew is leaving Saturday morning, and Jeff and Christine still need their washer and dryer hooked up. There's this huge punch list of these tiny little things all over the place... a leak in the bathroom and flooring to be finished. We just need help. We're so tired. There's so much to do, and I wanted them in their house by Thanksgiving."

We all prayed together, and I felt the weight of my burden release. This group understood. We'd worked shoulder to shoulder since the storm. But the most amazing part of this new family was their faith, the way they sought God's wisdom in prayer before they did anything. And when they prayed, mountains moved.

Each of my friends hugged me and encouraged me. I felt lighter driving away from our meeting that day, all tearful and refreshed. Beth sent Bible verses to fortify me.

One hour later, I'd parked in Jeff and Christine's driveway. Then I received a call from an unknown number in Florida. After I swiped right to answer, the man on the line said, "Hey, Courtney. I spoke to you some time back. I'm on my way right now. I'll be there Saturday morning. I'm the carpenter who does flip houses, and I'm coming to help you finish your punch list at Jeff and Christine's."

Of course he was.

My lip trembled, and I nodded, whispering my thanks to God. I hadn't remembered this particular volunteer was coming. My schedules and notes and building details were so jumbled. With my head bursting from overtime burnout, I couldn't remember much of anything.

But God knew. It was on His timeline, and wasn't this His plan anyway? The Lord was reminding me, once again, that He was the one in charge. It wasn't about me. Would I ever learn?

"Thank You, God," I whispered again.

Then Christine tapped on my window, her forehead wrinkled and her lips pursed.

I lowered the window, and a blast of cold air hit my face.

"Courtney, do you know of anyone who has electric heaters?" she asked.

Their HVAC system still wasn't finished. All the heat pump companies in our area were inundated with orders and falling behind. Too many needs, not enough installers.

I bit my lip. "We had so many donated just two months ago, but I don't know where they all went. Let me see what I can find."

"Okay. Well, we really need two or three. It's so cold trying to work in there."

"I know. I'm so sorry."

Christine went back inside their house, and I unlocked my phone. First, I called the church secretary. She said every donated heater in our fellowship hall had been given away. So I kept scrolling through my phone, trying to remember the names and numbers of other churches who'd been collecting supplies. I selected the name of one of my contacts and held the phone up to my mouth, doing talk-to-text.

"Hey. Do you know if anyone still has..." I started.

But as I was speaking, a truck plowed into the lot next to me, fifty yards away. A guy jumped out, unlocked a storage container in the middle of the field, and began unloading something into his truck bed. I squinted and looked more closely. They were heaters. Dozens of them. I bark-laughed, jumped out of the car, and trotted across the field to his truck.

"Hey! Do you have any extra heaters?" I called out over the cold wind.

"Yes, ma'am. I do. It's getting cold. I'm about to deliver these to some of the people in the mountains. The Buddy heaters are for people still sleeping in tents," he explained since these particular heaters were propane powered. His house was across the street. He'd been adopted by a church but was still waiting on the floors to be replaced and a new heat pump. Instead of licking his wounds, he was out helping others in the community.

"How about electric heaters? Do you have any of those?" I held my breath.

He rummaged around through supplies. "Yep. Looks like I have three."

Of course he did.

CHAPTER ELEVEN

The Friday before Thanksgiving, I conceded we'd miss our goal to get Jerry back in his house before the holiday. The thought pained me. The apartment where he was staying was only available until the week of Christmas. It was cold and snowy, and we were running out of time.

That afternoon, I got a call from another flood victim, the granddaughter of the man in the wheelchair. They were having their home rebuilt by the Kentucky crew. But their project was still months out, and they were staying in a nearby trailer with family. Where they were living, the heat pump had gone out. Everyone was cold. She asked if there was any way we could find them some heaters too.

Michael Marcum had delivered some kerosene heaters to their place to keep them warm for the time being. But it just wasn't enough.

"My papaw is cold. And I can't sleep for worrying about him." Her voice cracked.

"Surely there must be something we can do," I said to my husband that night. Then I texted our rebuilding crew to tell them I was going to head to their trailer the next morning to rummage around and see what could be done.

Adam Stine met me there. He'd fixed the insulation and underpinning on several damaged local trailers. He'd become an expert on the how-to. And although this wasn't a flood-impacted structure, this family was cold, and we wanted to help.

I was reminded of the verse in Isaiah 58:6–9a:

> Is this not the fast that I choose: to loose the bonds of wickedness, to undo the straps of the yoke, to let the oppressed go free, and to break every yoke? Is it not to share your bread with the hungry and bring the homeless poor

into your house; when you see the naked, to cover him, and not to hide yourself from your own flesh? Then shall your light break forth like the dawn, and your healing shall spring up speedily; your righteousness shall go before you; the glory of the Lord shall be your rear guard. Then you shall call, and the Lord will answer; you shall cry, and He will say, "Here I am."

"I can show you what needs to be done." Adam wiped his brow. "But I'm afraid I can't help today."

"That's okay." I dug out my gloves, crouched, and tugged on a piece of bent underpinning. "Just explain the gist of it, please."

Temperatures had climbed near fifty, but a drizzling rain was carrying in the next cold front. Snow was forecast for the following day. After Adam unloaded some rakes he'd brought, we crawled underneath the trailer. Animals had ripped out most of the trailer's insulation. The underpinning was missing on one side. So until that was repaired, animals would continue to get underneath.

"We may have some extra insulation." He sat back on his knees. "And I have some insulation pins too. I'll bring them back shortly."

"Awesome. Thank you, Adam!"

Adam stopped at the edge of the yard and turned to me. "You're just going to do this all by yourself?" he asked.

I shrugged. Surely God would give me the strength. Who was I to go home and sleep in my warm bed, knowing some family out there was freezing tonight?

"Okay. I'll be back." He waved and jogged back to his truck.

I began cleaning out the debris from underneath the trailer... the old insulation, a couple of dead animals. Which I can't pretend didn't freak me out. I *did* scream and do the heebie-jeebies dance.

"Courtney?" someone called from the yard not ten minutes later.

I scooted to the edge and peeked out. One of my volunteers from Jeff and Christine's house was standing there, a middle-aged woman from Iowa.

"What are you doing here?" I asked. I'd put out the call for more help, but I knew she was busy doing other things. Indoor things. "This is not fun work."

"I know. But I'm not about to let you do it by yourself. Let's tackle this together." She climbed under the trailer with me.

In minutes, Adam was back to help. And he brought Scott from his church. Ten minutes after that, three more men showed up. And then another guy who'd helped at Jerry's house came too.

Half an hour later, everyone's hair was full of cobwebs and spiders. We were itchy, covered in dirt and insulation. A couple of the pipes underneath the house were leaking, so we were a bit muddy too. Blessedly, one of the men on the job had plumbing experience—of course he did.

By lunchtime, it was pouring cold rain, but the four of us remaining sat beneath the trailer in the dirt, telling God stories and sharing our testimonies. We confessed struggles and praised Him for all He'd done.

When I left that afternoon, the trailer was fully insulated underneath, and underpinning was installed. But more important than the insulation, every worker had gleaned a gift of peace and love that day. I was so moved, I made a video talking about how God shows up not in majestic, ornate cathedrals but in the filth. Under a trailer. In a storm.

I also spoke to my Facebook followers about this family and my hope that they would be warmer now.

A few days later, I was sitting in Lori's office at the church building, going through mail and opening packages from all over the United States. She was printing checks for me to take to various places to pay for building materials.

"Oh, hey, by the way"—she leaned in, reading her computer screen—"I got an email from this lady who said she was sending a thousand-dollar check. She wants it to go for a heat pump for the trailer on Second Street."

I shook my head. "The..." I bit my lip. "What?"

Lori scrolled with her mouse. "Exactly. That's what I was wondering. What's the trailer on Second Street? You guys aren't working on Second Street."

My heart stopped. "That's the trailer we insulated last week... but I..." I couldn't talk. I swallowed. "Lori, I made a video about it, but I never, ever mentioned the name of the street where their trailer was. Are they local?"

She checked her email again. "Nope. She lives in South Carolina."

"So how did she know the name of the street—?" Chills raced up and down my spine.

Tears shimmered in Lori's eyes. "We both know the answer to that."

"But it's only a thousand. An HVAC unit will be way more than that. What do we do?"

"I think God's telling us to order a heat pump for those people in the cold trailer. I say we obey."

CHAPTER TWELVE

Once we'd ordered the heat pump for them, the funds multiplied to cover the cost. With every dime we spent, the account was replenished. For months, we never even checked the flood-relief balance at the church before we ordered materials or took on a new project. We knew God would provide. And provide He did.

Jeff and Christine had moved back into their bedroom, at least. They continued to wait on cabinets and the rest of their kitchen plumbing to be complete. They only had one working sink—in their laundry room. But at least they were out of the camper and in their new bed, which was another of God's miracles.

The Tuesday before Thanksgiving, I received a call from a volunteer in Michigan, John. He'd been blowing up my phone, itching to come and volunteer. But the only days he could come were Thanksgiving Day and Black Friday. We were all burned-out and exhausted, including the homeowners. Jeff and Christine and Jerry had all said they were looking forward to a couple of days of downtime with no volunteers in their homes or even on the street. Just peace and quiet.

So, when John's name popped up on my phone screen, I wasn't sure why he was calling. I'd already told him not to come. I was standing in Jeff and Christine's living room when I answered.

"Hey, Courtney. It's John again. I'm sorry to bother you. I know you said you didn't really need help this week, but I wanted to call and check one more time."

I looked at Jeff and Christine. "Hang on, John."

I muted the phone and faced Jeff and Christine. "This is the guy from Michigan who was wanting to come and help on Thanksgiving Day and Black Friday. Do you guys still want to be left alone?"

"No!" Christine's eyes bulged. "We changed our minds. He can come."

John was elated, so I gave him their number to work out the details.

The day before Thanksgiving, I met with a larger church in town to speak to their group about donating to the work. I'd met a deacon from their group in the most peculiar way... exiting the polls on Election Day. I'd gone to vote wearing my paint clothes, which spawned a conversation in the parking lot. Soon, the two of us were excitedly discussing God's relief work in our area.

"We have some extra funds! Would you be willing to come and speak to our deacons about the work in Hampton?" he asked.

"Absolutely!" I agreed.

And so I did. That Wednesday, November 27, I spoke to their group about the different homes being adopted and what was needed. Namely, that week, we were desperate for two sets of appliances for two units another church had adopted. They were low on funds. I made my pleas, left, and prayed about it all the way home.

Thanksgiving Day, we posted Jeff and Christine's Amazon wish list. Within three days, every single item had been purchased and sent either to their home or to the church building. God's family was doing it again.

I tried to get Jeff and Christine and John to come to our house for Thanksgiving dinner. We were already hosting Jerry and about thirty other folks. But they declined, and someone from our church ended up delivering plates of food to them. John was the new favorite volunteer.

"He is wonderful!" Christine gushed on the phone the next day. "He's been putting in the vanity and the lights and working on trim. He hasn't stopped since he got here."

Sunday night, my husband and I were talking about our prayer list. We kept an ongoing war-room prayer list of the needs in our family, folks who were sick or needed spiritual help, and personal situations and finances.

"So what do we need to pray about tonight?" Paul asked.

"We need another John." I sighed and sank onto our bed.

"Another John?" Paul tilted his head.

"Yes! John was amazing this week. I'm sad he's gone. He accomplished so much, and he had every skill set we needed. There is still so much on the punch lists for Jeff and Christine and for Jerry."

I'd hardly finished my sentence when my husband lowered his head, closed his eyes, and prayed, "Dear God, we need another John."

I giggled, and he opened one eye and looked at me. He was being serious. I dipped my head and closed my eyes again, chagrined.

The next morning at 10:30 a.m., I received a call from John.

"John!" I squealed. "We were just praying about you last night. We were praying God would send us another John!" I moved an oversized throw pillow so I could sit on the couch.

"Actually, that's why I'm calling," he said.

"Oh, yeah?"

"Yeah." He paused. "I think I'm about to buy a bus."

I snorted. "Did you say a bus?"

"Yes. Well, I'm still praying about it, but I'm rounding up other skilled carpenters and volunteers. If I can get this bus, we can fit twenty on it and all come down there to work."

Ten minutes later, my husband walked into the room. I was still sitting on the couch, crying.

"What is it now?" He rubbed my shoulder.

I could hardly get the words out. "God's not sending us another John. He's sending twenty Johns."

Then I went to make a video to tell everyone about how awesome our God is. My husband and I were learning yet another lesson throughout this entire process: We couldn't be too specific or too persistent when it came to our prayers. God heard every massive and tiny need.

"The righteous cry out, and the Lord hears, and delivers them out of their troubles" (Psalm 34:17).

CHAPTER THIRTEEN

The first week of December, all the furniture was delivered for both Jeff and Christine's house and Jerry's house. Who could believe it had been just over two months since the flood when I'd stood with Jerry in his yard, staring at the missing back wall of his entire house? Or since Jeff and Christine had spent hours stranded on their bed with their dog in the rising floodwaters? But here we were... nearing the end of God's divine shower of blessings covering these households.

December 6, I was standing in Jerry's living room, watching the volunteer electrician hang ceiling fans. Jerry's kitchen cabinets and countertops were done. Another Christian man had donated a dump trailer for the front yard to collect construction scraps. Fingerprints of God's love were pressed all over this project.

Then, as I drove down the street to Jeff and Christine's, more of the Lord's work stood out. I passed two different homes where other churches were paying to have heat pumps put in for families. A volunteer contractor worked at someone else's house. Jeff and Christine's house was finished except for the dishwasher. God had mended the hurts and met every need on this street. And those were only the parts I could see on the outside. Not to mention the restored souls who turned their lives over to Him through the tribulation.

A few hours later, an unknown caller popped up on my phone. It was a local man I didn't know. Someone had given him my number, and he was calling to relay that he had six sets of brand-new washers and dryers to donate. We didn't need them on this street, but we would need them for the folks in the valley where Curtis and Desie were working.

"We are storing them right now, and we mostly just need them gone," the man on the phone told me.

"Um. Okay." I reached for my notebook and took a seat at my desk. "I guess you can bring them to our house and put them in our garage."

We had no other current solution. And the Kentucky crew was rebuilding three homes now. They could use three of the sets. Besides, I was sure God had some plan I didn't know about. At this point, the less I knew, the better. God was the ultimate planner. Not me.

At 1:30 that same day, one of our volunteers posted in our group. We'd set up a connection point in the Signal app for every adopting church of every home on the street. It was a great place to share info, resources, and volunteers.

Does anyone know where we can get more porta potties? the post asked.

TEMA (Tennessee Emergency Management Agency) had set porta potties down the street two weeks after the flood. But then they showed up the first week of December and took all of them without warning.

We didn't want to pay for six new porta potties, but I sent the group the name of a reliable local company I knew. Pottybox Portables. Porta potties were a necessity.

About 4:30 that day, two men showed up at my house with a truck and trailer full of washers and dryers. I helped the guys unload everything into my garage, and, of course, I couldn't keep my mouth shut about the God stories and interventions I'd witnessed these last months.

One man reached into his pocket and pulled out a business card. "Hey, by the way, my name is Blake, and I own Pottybox Portables. If any of your crews need porta potties, I'll be happy to provide them for free until the project is complete. Just let me know."

And here he was standing in my garage three hours after I'd seen that post in the Signal app.

I giggle-cried while the men looked at me like I'd lost my mind. I doubled over and dabbed at my eyes, trying to get my emotions under control. Because seriously. Who cries over porta potties?

God provided again. I couldn't wait to post in the Signal app and tell all the other coordinators about the porta potties from God.

*

December 9, I met Jerry at my work office so he could open the hundreds of Amazon boxes folks had sent him back in October. He had everything from dish towels and pillows to a slow cooker and cleaning supplies. Yet the best part about the big Amazon-box-opening party wasn't the gifts. It was notes from hundreds of people all over the country. Some shared Scriptures. Others wrote personal notes to Jerry, telling of the prayers they'd sent up for him. And still others just signed their names and their state.

When we finished, we had several overflowing carts of housewares to be wheeled outside, plus a huge pile of flattened cardboard boxes. Jerry sat at my desk, the hundreds of tiny notes from packages spread in front of him.

He folded his hands and blinked teary eyes. "I don't deserve any of this. Why was I so blessed?"

I couldn't speak; I could only shake my head.

But I was beginning to think I knew why. God was using this horrible storm to bring hope and unity to His people. He was igniting revival in our community and softening hearts on a global level. Just like He always did, God was taking what the devil meant for evil and using it for good.

As Jerry sat there behind my desk, looking over his new household items, I couldn't help but think back to the framing crew who had come to rebuild his house the second week after the flood. They told me his home would have collapsed in two to three years due to rot and decay. Now he had a brand-new, beautiful home. All new fixtures. New furniture.

While the gifts of God's family could never replace Jerry's unthinkable loss after Hurricane Helene, they fortified him nonetheless. He was moving back into his home, yes. And he'd made hundreds of new friends (and fans) along the way—not to mention the beautiful testimony he'd gained to share with others.

*

December 11, I hit another wall. Not a spiritual wall this time, but a physical wall. My body gave out, and I was as sick as I've ever been. I lost my voice and lay in bed for days, checking messages and trying to keep the work going, though I couldn't be on the jobsites.

And wouldn't you know it? The work didn't need me at all. God kept moving the needle while I was down.

On December 13, the local church I'd met with the day before Thanksgiving reached out to let me know they'd changed their mind about providing two sets of appliances for those units on Clearwater Street. My terrible cough and raging fever didn't keep my temper at bay. I admit, I was furious. Theirs was such a large church, and I didn't understand why the smallest churches with the biggest faith were the ones carrying the entire load. (If only I'd stopped to remind myself of the story of David and Goliath.)

God's Word was full of examples of the little people, the little groups, the insignificant. These were the tools God used to carry out His plan. He didn't need massive armies or strong leaders. He merely used the willing.

"But God chose what is foolish in the world to shame the wise; God chose what is weak in the world to shame the strong" (I Corinthians 1:27).

Of course, in my angry state, I wasn't focused on any of this. I was being human again. After the call, I collapsed into my pillow. Then I turned off my ringer and fell sound asleep.

Two hours later, I startled awake. My ringer was still off, but my phone screen lit up and displayed the contact for one of our volunteers from South Carolina who'd helped with Jerry's house. Half awake and groggy, I answered anyway.

The lady on the other end, now a dear friend, was so encouraging. She told me I needed the rest and sometimes, when we don't take the time to take care of ourselves, we get sick. When I started venting about the appliance situation, she chuckled.

"That's actually why I'm calling," she said. "My husband and I just sold a piece of land and wanted to donate. We live near a Lowe's outlet with appliances too. If you want, we can go ahead and purchase what's needed for the duplex and have it delivered the day after Christmas."

Of course she could.

The next day, one of my Facebook followers sent me a package of immune revival supplies. I was on antibiotics and still trying to run the world from the comfort of my bed. I didn't tell anyone, but I was also fighting severe anxiety. I couldn't sleep at night. I was on such a spiritual high, but battling my head nonetheless, like I was on the front lines of spiritual warfare.

While I was sick, the calamities persisted. Jerry's house still wasn't finished. Just after his power was connected, the guys doing the gutters pulled in, snagged the line with their truck, and yanked the electrical connection off the house. It blew a transformer and wiped out the whole street. He didn't have a mattress yet either.

We continued to pray for God to work things out, and Jerry did finally move back in on December 18. It was one week before Christmas, mere days before his time was up at the apartment where he'd been staying. And I thought back to Paul's prayer that first night, for God to please let us get Jerry back in his house by Christmas.

*

A few days later, another Facebook follower messaged me. She said she'd been praying for me and felt led to share a song with me. It was "Still Waters" by Leanna Crawford. The song is all about fighting anxiety by quoting Psalm 23 and how Scripture can pull you out of the darkest places. I cried so hard the first time I listened to it. It felt like God was telling me to hang in there, to meditate on His word, and to trust Him when I was feeling uncertain.

I wish I could remember the name of the person who sent me the song, but it became my favorite, my battle song. I listened to it on repeat continuously and shared it with friends. Whenever I felt anxious, I played "Still Waters" and was prompted to rest in God's promises. Those words from Psalm 23 carried me through.

CHAPTER FOURTEEN

On December 20, we had a special dinner at our house with Curtis and Desie. We wanted to hear more about their workload and what they needed. God was still sending building materials, campers, funds, vehicles, and work crews. He obviously wasn't quitting anytime soon, though our time with Jeff and Christine and Jerry was wrapping up.

"It's been challenging in Valley Forge," Curtis told us. "We haven't had much help."

He and his wife had finished a number of homes on their own, working six days a week and using their own tools. Occasionally, they would have crews come in from our church or even out of state. Keith, a deacon from our church, had been integral in organizing workdays to help Curtis and

Desie. It was a huge undertaking, though. Way too many homes for this handful of volunteers.

I scribbled out notes on the addresses and information of each homeowner, along with what was needed. Some homes were nearly complete, lacking only the installation of kitchen cabinets. Others still required a massive overhaul.

"There's one I'd really like you and Paul to take a look at," Curtis said. "It's Frank and Mindy's, and it's in pretty bad shape."

The next day, Paul and I drove down to Valley Forge to see the progress. We were eager to jump in and get started... until we reached River Road. Then we both fell silent, and I covered my mouth, holding in the emotion. The scene out the truck window was like going back in time two months. There were pieces of cars and boats in trees. Plenty of makeshift campers housing cold families. And very little progress.

Curtis was right. This area hadn't received the masses of volunteers with excavation equipment or the entire churches adopting homes. Not like the street where we'd been working. Curtis and Desie had been tackling this load mostly by themselves. This was so much bigger than Paul and I anticipated.

We parked in the driveway at Frank and Mindy's house. The situation didn't look too grim out front. The interior of the home was a different story. The structure's entire back half was sinking and bowed, like its center might snap in half at any moment. The home had been stripped to the studs from three feet down, but the entire place needed a sound gutting. The back of the home would have to be removed and rebuilt. With the foundation damage, the roofline made a *U*.

My husband measured while I recorded videos and made notes for him. This project was just as big as Jerry's, if not bigger. My insides twisted as I scuffled along mud-caked floors. This couple was living with family twenty minutes away. They had waited hopelessly for three months with no progress on their home, and they couldn't afford to rebuild. Their story was a common tale. They didn't have flood insurance because they didn't even live in a floodplain. I couldn't imagine how overwhelmed they felt.

Frank, the homeowner, had told Curtis, "Just get me some drywall and insulation. I'll figure out how to put everything back together. And I don't need cabinets. I can just do a countertop and some studs to brace it."

When Curtis told us that, Paul let out a breath and held up a hand. "God's going to build a brand-new, beautiful home," he said. "God doesn't do the bare minimum."

We stepped out on the front porch, and a new burden weighed on my shoulders. I understood why God was only lighting our path one foot at a time. He knew we couldn't handle the big picture. He was only feeding us what we could chew for the time being. And here we were, opening up for a great big bite.

"How much do we have left in the flood-relief fund?" Paul asked after we got back in the truck.

"Um. I don't know. Let me text Lori." I knocked the mud off my boots and closed the door. Just as I opened my phone, a text came in from Lori. Of course.

She'd written: *Would you believe we had over $5,000 come in the mail just today?*

I passed my phone to my husband so he could read it too.

"Okay, God," I whispered. "We hear You. You're here, and we're going to keep moving."

As we pulled to the stop sign at the end of their drive, a lump grew in my throat, and chills raced down my arms and legs. I started sobbing.

"What is it now?" Paul reached for my hand, smiling at me.

"Frank and Mindy's house. This road..." I couldn't speak, pointing to the road sign.

"Yes?"

"It's Stillwater. Their home is on Stillwater Circle. Stillwater. That's like the song I've had on replay for the last week, the song someone sent me. 'Still Waters.'"

God was calling us to rebuild the home on Stillwater Road. I shook my head. It was another sign.

*

The next day, I read through Facebook messages for four hours, and wouldn't you know it? Every single item needed for Frank and Mindy's remodel miraculously appeared. We had twenty-three volunteers coming from New York, Ohio, and Pennsylvania. Someone else was donating appliances. Two different families were forgoing the exchange of Christmas gifts to send more funds to the church so the work could continue.

And then I had one message from another lady, a local who had gone through the flood. She was a widow, all alone. And she was inquiring if I could find two heaters for her cold home.

I opened the Signal app to post in our group. But before I could type out the message, Ryan Vernon posted a photo of some of the leftover supplies from a truckload of materials that week. They'd been sorting and delivering as needed.

He'd captioned it with the question: *Do you guys know anyone who could use these?*

It was a picture of two heaters.

CHAPTER FIFTEEN

Our work in the Valley Forge area wasn't limited to Frank and Mindy's renovation. We were also helping Curtis and Desie finish the other homes already under construction. The first priority? Getting Jack moved back into his house. Jack was a retired veteran in his seventies, and his home-repair needs were like many others we'd seen. After the storm damage, his home was gutted down to studded walls only. He needed insulation, drywall, flooring, a new bathroom and kitchen, all appliances, including a washer and dryer, and some new windows.

Two of the ladies from our church were helping him with his Amazon list. He would require all new furniture in addition to hundreds of replacement household items. Jack was a character. He loved teasing the volunteers, carrying around his lapdog, Cocoa, and chiding us while we worked. Naturally, he was antsy to be back in his home. He'd lived there his entire life. But he sure did have a great attitude about his predicament.

We were planning a big "paint party" for Jack on December 27. Several volunteers (both locally and out of state) had already committed to help. Then we had a crew of ten coming in from Kentucky two days after that to put down flooring and trim. But the day before our little paint party, the drywall crew called to say they wouldn't be finished in time.

I was beyond frustrated. My plans were always scheduled on double time, in fifth gear. It was a lifelong character flaw I battled. I was a mover and a pusher, not a sitter or a waiter. It made me impatient and cranky and bossy at times, I admit. But construction work timelines were seldom reliable, and I had to deal with it.

Of course, it never occurred to me that God had something bigger and better in mind for December 27.

That night, I ranted to my husband while I checked Facebook messages. The donations were still coming, as were the work crews. I was trying to contact everyone who'd agreed to help paint Jack's house to let them know the workday was canceled. I also received a message from a local man who owned a car dealership and repair shop. He'd fixed up a vehicle and wanted to provide it to a family in need. I told him I didn't know of anyone at the moment, but I would be on the lookout. Most of the families of the adopted homes had already received vehicles.

The next day, on what should have been our paint day, a group of nine men came in from Mississippi to deliver a refurbished camper. My lead contact on the project, a man in his seventies named Dan, had been communicating with me for a month. He wanted his team to drive in, do a complete setup for the camper, and build a cover over it. They were building a deck and stairs on it too... something reliable and convenient for up to a year while the family rebuilt their home.

Dan's team arrived in Bumpus Cove that morning. We hadn't yet visited the hard-hit area about thirty minutes from where we'd been rebuilding. Covered up with the projects in Hampton and Valley Forge, we hadn't taken the time to go. But several of our friends were working there, and my husband was helping lay out two house plans for another church to do rebuilds. His project manager, Keith Ellis, was coordinating those efforts.

"I was heading to Bumpus Cove today anyway," Paul told me. "Why don't you go with me? You can meet Dan and the guys and see the other new builds Keith is doing."

I agreed, not knowing what God had in store. We took several detours on our way in Paul's truck, navigating around closed roads and bridges. When we crossed the last bridge and turned into the valley, we were in shock. While there were still unbelievable piles of debris and destruction, there was also desolation—entire masses of land where the river had spread and overpowered the banks, taking trees, property, and homes.

There was simply nothing left but a giant gully between the mountains. Nine homes on one side of the river had been swept away. And what's more: there was no land left to rebuild. The flood had taken it all.

We drove on. Soon, the road ended, and we met a makeshift mound of riprap and gravel. It was one lane alongside the river, hugging the mountain, to a steep drop-off below. Trucks and road crews were still hauling in gravel. I'd heard about this place, the community that became an island, cut off from the rest of the world after the flood hit. Seeing it in person was sobering.

Beyond the makeshift land bridge, we found the Mississippi crew. They were setting up sawhorses and getting to work. The camper was already in place in front of a home that sat back on its haunches, like it might just tip over and give up its ghost any moment. The front yard overlooked a vast expanse of treeless silt with the shrunken river trickling through its center. This could've been what the world looked like just after creation. No people. No power lines or roads. Just open, raw wilderness—a canvas Hurricane Helene had wiped blank. When a biting wind stole across the river, I turned my head and zipped my jacket up to my chin.

"Courtney?" A man with thick white hair and a beard waved to me. His voice took flight on another frigid gust.

"Yes, sir," I called back. "Are you Dan?"

He widened his smile, seemingly unfazed by the elements. He strode toward me and pulled me into a bear hug. Then he chuckled and dabbed at his eyes. "Girl, it is so good to finally meet you! Isn't God good?"

I loved him. Instantly.

Dan called his volunteers to circle up and pray. Several of the men were crying by the time he finished. They were thrilled for the opportunity to drive thirteen hours with this camper and work in the bitter cold to serve someone in need.

Theirs was a miraculous example of God's family uniting to serve others. I watched them tearfully, my heart swelling.

The scene reminded me of the verses from Matthew 25:37–40:

> Then the righteous will answer Him, saying, "Lord, when did we see you hungry and feed you, or thirsty and give you drink? And when did we see you a stranger and welcome you, or naked and clothe you? And when did we see you sick and in prison and visit you?" And the King will answer them, "Truly, I say to you, as you did it to one of the least of these my brothers, you did it to me."

After we said goodbye to our new friends from Mississippi, we headed back to the main road in Bumpus Cove, where Paul was drawing out a few modifications on two complete rebuilds. We ended up staying there for a couple of hours. One of the men helping manage the project came to Paul's truck window to talk to us. He shared his stories of their struggles in the area, how they hadn't experienced much help at all. He also mentioned there'd been corruption—thieves coming in to steal supplies from those who'd lost everything and out-of-staters posing as flood victims to receive donations. It was a heartbreaking story.

"There are still too many needs to count." The man shook his head.

"Like what?" I piped up. "What can we do to help?"

The man raised one eyebrow. "Know anybody who wants to donate a car?"

My chin trembled, and I struggled to form the words. "Actually, I do."

The man's eyes widened. "Seriously?"

"Seriously. Someone messaged me last night wanting to donate a car." Goose bumps rose on my arms.

"The elderly lady next door lost everything. She sure could use a car."

I nodded. Of course she could. That was the whole reason the drywallers were delayed, the reason our paint day was canceled. God sent us to Bumpus Cove to talk to this man so the sweet lady next door, who'd been praying for a car, could receive her miracle.

I cried all the way home on the bumpy roads and detours, repenting once again for trying to do things according to my plan and my timeline, for being impatient while God was working out something better.

*

December 31, we finally got our paint day at Mr. Jack's. A man drove in from Indiana to help us. Another lady came from the Pigeon Forge area. Plus, six or seven members from our church joined in.

The mood inside the house was light and upbeat. Strangers made conversation and laughed together. Mr. Jack walked around with his dog Cocoa in hand, inspecting our work and teasing us.

That afternoon, I was on a ladder in the kitchen when I heard someone knocked on the front door. Keith Carr, the deacon from our church who'd been helping Curtis and Desie, had told me a lady might be stopping by to meet us.

"She said something about a donation," Keith whispered.

The lady came into the kitchen and looked around. "I just wanted to come down here for myself and see the work being done," she explained.

I nodded, understanding that. There were so many scammers out there, claiming to do relief work and collecting funds or materials for themselves. I told her about some of the miracles we'd witnessed and the momentum as we moved into phase two of the recovery efforts here. Keith showed her around the house and explained about the other works in progress down the street.

Before the lady left, she wrote a check to our church for twelve thousand dollars. Lori was painting in the next room, so she took the check to be deposited. And as I stood there on my ladder in the kitchen, trimming out near the ceiling, I shook my head and prayed, struggling to see my brushstrokes through the tears. Here was one more reason our paint day December 27 was delayed. God placed us in this house today to meet this lady.

Jack's entire house was primed and painted in one day, and we weren't behind at all.

CHAPTER SIXTEEN

"Hey, Courtney! This is Shane," a man on the phone said.

"Shane! Hi!"

Shane was the son-in-law of Dan, my sweet Mississippi friend who brought in the camper. Shane was part of Dan's setup team that day, along with his two sons, Cody and Tanner. They had a booming business in their area doing custom kitchen cabinets and other carpentry work.

Shane sucked in a deep breath. "Listen. I want to talk to you about something, and I'm almost scared to say it. But I know God wants me to step out in faith and just trust Him."

"I know that feeling." I chuckled. "What is it?"

"Me and my boys want to commit to doing the custom kitchen cabinets, doors, and trim in every new house you guys decide to take on."

My mouth fell open. The kitchen cabinets, doors, and trim were the projects no one wanted. It was the end-of-the-road punch-list stuff. And it took serious carpentry skill. This phone call was such an answer to prayers. I explained to Shane about Frank and Mindy's house first. Then I sent him Paul's drawing for their kitchen layout. Another house, two doors down from theirs, also needed their preordered kitchen cabinets hung and trim put down.

"Let us know when you'll be ready," Shane told me.

"Only God knows that." I laughed. "But it looks like we have twenty-three volunteers coming in the next few weeks. Who knows how far we'll get."

That afternoon, I went by Jack's house, where our crew from Kentucky was putting down flooring and painting trim. There was an atmosphere of joy and revival, just like every other construction site. No matter the difficulty of the task, volunteers shared their testimonies and Scriptures with each other. They prayed and loved on the homeowners. Revival was rampant.

*

Even though Paul and I were no longer working on the street where we started, many other churches and volunteers were still finishing up there. And for as long as the work continued, the Tuesday meetings continued. Our crew was spread thin, though. So on Tuesday, January 2, Adam and I were the only meeting attendees at Dunkin' Donuts in Hampton, less than a mile from all the worksites.

We reviewed the itinerary for the day's meeting, noting minor decisions to make. But mostly, we just shared our God stories from the last weeks. As we talked, several of the homeowners from Clearwater Street came in. Visiting with them, listening to their stories, and hugging their necks warmed our hearts.

"I do have one request I just found out about yesterday," Adam said.

I leaned in.

"A lady in Roan Mountain needs a camper. She lost everything months ago, and now her temporary housing has fallen through," he explained.

"I should check my messages," I joked. "God's probably already sent the camper, and it's just waiting in my inbox."

We both laughed.

That afternoon, I read through Facebook messages for a couple of hours. And guess what? A lady from North Carolina had sent a message the day before.

Do you have someone who needs a camper?

*

That first week of January, we ordered a few more of those donated porta potties for the remaining construction sites on River Road. We also organized a paint party for another home just down the road from Frank and Mindy's. Things were moving right along. I kept having folks message me about the week of February 10. It was like God was sending every building material and every worker for that one week.

January 7, before our nightly prayer, my husband and I talked about some families who'd already been helped. We counted up five different households who had lost their faith before the flood. Some of them struggled with wounds from old church hurt. Others didn't believe in God anymore.

All five of those families were back in church. If you met them in their front yard or asked about the progress on their home, they bubbled over with their own stories of God's miracles. Their lives had taken complete one-eighties, not because of their new homes and new furniture or the trauma after the devastation. Rather, they were transformed by God's love softening their hearts and filling their souls.

I told my husband good night, but I didn't close my eyes. There was too much to think about, and my heart was so full. I thanked God for allowing us the privilege to be a tiny part of His master plan.

CHAPTER SEVENTEEN

By January 13, one home in the Valley Forge area was ready for paint. But the holidays were over, and winter was upon us. The kids were back in school, and we didn't have an army of volunteers show up for our little paint day. It was just me at first, and then Keith's wife, Melissa, came. We started with the ceilings, just the two of us. And if you've ever painted ceilings, you understand the physical agony.

Around 2:00 p.m., we stopped to stretch. I rubbed my neck and surveyed the progress—or, uh, lack thereof.

"This is impossible." I swigged another sip of my energy drink. "I don't know how we'll get it done."

Too bad we didn't have the same crew that had finished Jack's house in one day.

It was Monday. We had a work team coming in from Ohio to install flooring on Thursday. We needed the whole house painted before then. To make matters more complicated, the homeowner had requested dark paint colors in most of the house. It was going to take at least two coats after the primer, in addition to the ceilings.

I felt weak and defeated, spread thin. If it hadn't been so cold and dirty, I could have spread out on the floor and gone sound asleep. We were still struggling to keep our home life/work life/relief work balance.

I sank onto a box of flooring in the living room and retrieved my paint-speckled phone.

"Maybe God will send us a painter." I chuckled.

The number of unread text messages on my screen was ridiculous. But I just didn't have the capacity to do the work and take care of the family and keep the businesses going and reply to messages. I scrolled, feeling depressed.

And then my finger stopped on a message I'd received at 10:00 p.m. the night before from "Tom the Skilled Carpenter from Oklahoma." (I had to save everyone's contact info with specific notes so I could remember who was who.)

"Melissa..." I covered my mouth and read the message aloud. I'd forgotten this guy was even coming to help.

Tom said he was driving his box truck all the way from Oklahoma, full of the tools he would need. And he was already on the road. He would be ready to work on Wednesday morning.

I replied and asked if he could help paint. He said he would be glad to. Sure enough, by 8:00 a.m. Wednesday morning, he was on a ladder painting the living room. And the whole place was ready for flooring by Thursday, right on schedule.

Tom stayed eight days and finished multiple projects on that house. He took care of plumbing issues and hung light fixtures, in addition to his supreme paint job. And every time we presented "just one more project," Tom had the skill set to do it. He was a reinforcement sent from the Lord.

On January 16, we posted Jack's Amazon wish list link. His home was nearing completion, minus those last-minute projects still hanging over us. Every single item on his list was purchased within twelve hours.

January 18, I received a call from Michael Marcum, the minister in Kentucky.

"Courtney, I have a problem, and I'm hoping you can help."

"Sure. What's up?"

"We're doing block on those homes on Clearwater Street, and we were planning to order from Builders First. But when I gave them our tax-exempt form, they said they can't accept it because it's from Kentucky. Can we run our purchases through your church? I'm sorry to bother you with this."

"It's no problem. I don't think our church has an account with Builders First, but let me call around and see what I can find out."

First, I called Lori, who confirmed we did *not* have an account at Builders First. Then I called Paul to ask his advice, but he said we would have to drive down there and physically set up a new account for the Kentucky guys to use our tax form.

"Ugh. We don't have time for that. Let me call Keith and see if he can go," I told him.

I hung up and dialed Keith.

"Hello," he answered on the fourth ring. He sounded busy.

"I'm sorry to bother you! Are you in the middle of something?"

"Mmm. Not really. Just leaving Builders First."

"Builders First? What are you doing there?"

"I decided to come down here this morning and get the church account set up with our tax-exempt card."

Of course he did.

We were able to order building materials for the Kentucky crew through our church's account that very day, and work continued as planned.

That evening, I received a call from a government person, Phil, who'd been trying to help flood survivors. Their group had come to us, asking for information on homeowners, determining who still needed what. But, as far as I knew, none of the applications had been approved, and no locals had been helped.

Every time Phil called, I dreaded answering. We were spinning our wheels with his team, yielding zero results, wasting our time. And honestly, I didn't want to work through them anyway. We were doing this for God to get the glory, not the government.

So cringing, I stepped away from the noise of our family room and into the quiet of our bedroom.

"I want to talk to you about the methods you're using to rebuild homes," Phil said.

"Okay…" I held my breath.

"The problem with what you're doing is that the fundraising will run out—"

"We're not fundraising," I interrupted him.

"What do you mean, you're not fundraising?"

"We're not fundraising."

"Then where are you getting all this money and supplies and labor?"

"God is our bank."

"So you *are* fundraising."

"No."

"Then why are people sending money?"

"We're just talking about what God's doing. We're sharing His miracles. And when people hear about what He's doing in our area, they want to come help. They want to be part of it."

"Well, what will you do when you run out of money? What happens then?"

"I guess that means God's done," I said. "None of this was our plan. It's not our timeline, and it's not our money. It's God's plan. He is our bank, and He is our resource. This is all by Him and for Him."

After we got off the phone, I sat on the edge of the bed. In every instance where a government organization tried to come in and help rebuild, the efforts were gridlocked. It fell through. There was so much time and unnecessary paperwork and red tape with no progress.

We were working on the seventh house God had rebuilt through our church in only four months. And there was no debt or paperwork. There were no empty promises or applications. Just hundreds of volunteers and supplies, hand-holding prayers in backyards, and folks sharing food and stories. God was rebuilding homes and feeding souls, all in one great big collective effort. No government assistance required, thank you very much.

I decided to stop taking Phil's calls after that. My time was better spent elsewhere.

CHAPTER EIGHTEEN

January 20, a charitable group in our area agreed to spend a cold, snow-covered day completing the demo work on Frank and Mindy's for us, free of charge. The entire back half of the house had to go. Temperatures plummeted into the teens, but we had a dozen or more volunteers show up to work.

When I stopped by to check their progress, I noticed quite a bit of standing water in the crawl space. It was probably eight inches deep. I informed our Valley Forge coordinators right away, which basically consisted of Keith and Curtis.

"We need a sump pump," Curtis told me.

"Okay." I made a note. "I'll see if I can pick up one from Lowe's this week."

This was a huge project, and there was so much work to be done. I wondered how many months this would take. The demolition crew was a timely blessing.

January 27, we had a professional, paid-for framing crew drive in for the week. A donor for the work had paid their salaries to help us. They were coming in from West Virginia to rebuild the entire back half of Frank and Mindy's house. Again, it was perfect timing. We had those twenty-three volunteer carpenters coming in around February 10. And the beautiful part about all of it? Besides us delivering lumber and checking in on the volunteers, these dedicated servants gave our team a much-needed break.

Curtis, Desie, Keith, Paul, and I were able to take some time off from the relief work to take care of personal things in our lives and businesses. I felt like God was showing us He didn't expect us to do all the work ourselves. He was giving us space to breathe and recover.

It reminded me of a Bible story during the Israelites' battle against the Amalekites in Exodus 17:11–13:

Whenever Moses held up his hand, Israel prevailed, and whenever he lowered his hand, Amalek prevailed. But Moses' hands grew weary, so they took a stone and put it under him, and he sat on it, while Aaron and Hur held up his hands, one on one side, and the other on the other side. So his hands were steady until the going down of the sun. And Joshua overwhelmed Amalek and his people with the sword.

God was sending our own personal Aaron and Hur teams to hold up our hands. He provided a rock for us to sit on until the battle was finished.

Because I had some time, I went back to work in our retail store for a couple of days. We owned a bin liquidation store, where we bought truckloads of overstock and return items. Then we dumped them in bins and priced them by the day. But the price of inventory was skyrocketing, and our sales numbers couldn't keep up. The devil was piling more stress on our plates.

The first day I was back in the store, we'd just restocked a truckload of new merchandise. I was discussing some logistics with our manager when I noticed a large box in the bins.

"What's that?" I stopped talking and stepped around him for a closer look.

"Can you believe it?" He chuckled. "We got a sump pump this week!"

I put one hand on my forehead and swallowed back the tears. Of course we did. God always took care of us in the relief work, and I was certain He would provide for us personally as well. It was another reminder of His everlasting promises.

I delivered the sump pump to Frank and Mindy's house the next day.

*

That night, as I was readying for bed, I received a text message from our group. Jack wasn't ready to move back in. I sighed and plugged in my phone as more messages poured in. There was still a huge list of to-be-finished projects. He needed his toilet set, closet racks in the closets so he could hang up his clothes, another kitchen cabinet hung, his vanity installed, and a window repaired. He'd moved a new twin bed back into his bedroom, but he didn't even have a functioning bathroom or kitchen.

"What's the matter?" my husband asked.

I flopped back onto my pillow and sighed. "I should have been a carpenter."

"What do you mean?"

I threw my hands up. "I don't know how to set a toilet or install vanities or any of this stuff! Jack's house isn't done. All of our Ohio guys are gone now. And Curtis and Keith are exhausted."

"So we should pray about it," my husband reminded me, in his calm, never-stressed tone.

We joined hands through our bedtime prayers, and then I fell asleep. But it was a restless night's sleep. I tossed and turned, stressed. At 2:00 a.m., I was wide awake, staring at the ceiling, praying.

"God, please send us all the people we need to do this punch list," I pled.

I was up by 4:30 and feeling refreshed, ready to go. By 7:00, texts and phone calls bombarded me, one on top of the other. Someone volunteered to do Jack's closets. Someone else sent a plumber.

Someone else said they could do the vanity. And by 10:30 a.m., I told Paul every single thing on the list had been taken care of.

I'd needlessly lost sleep, thinking once again this was somehow my project.

*

That week, Curtis called.

"Courtney, I have a prayer request," he said.

"Okay. Sure. What's up?"

"There's this guy off River Road, Randy. His home was in terrible shape. I've tried to help him some since the start of the flood, but he's done pretty much all the repair work on his own. Every time I tried to help or send volunteers, he told me to use them somewhere else. He never left his house. He just stayed there and slept in the mud from day one. He's been helping all of his neighbors too."

"Wow. That's incredible."

"Yes, it is. And his house is almost done now. I'm helping him hang kitchen cabinets this week. But there's something he needs, and he'd never ask for it."

"What's that?"

"He has a landscaping company, but he lost his truck, plus all of his landscaping tools, in the flood."

"That's terrible! Let's make him an Amazon wish list and see if people will get him the rest of what he needs. And we'll mention the truck too. Maybe God has something in mind."

I went down to Randy's house so I could meet him and do a video of the repairs he'd managed mostly on his own. He told me his story, how the floodwaters had rushed in and he'd climbed to the roof with his dog. After the waters receded, he stayed in his house with no electricity and bucketloads of mud. He camped there, having nowhere else to go. And he started working on repairs right away.

It later dawned on me. This was the same Randy who'd received a donated refrigerator from Poplar Ridge Christian Church. God had connected us at the beginning of the flood, and we didn't even know it.

I was impressed with his immaculate house. When I told him about making an Amazon wish list, he said he felt bad asking for help. I explained this was a blessing to the ones giving, that God's family *wanted* to help. I also told him we were praying for a truck to come any day now.

That afternoon, I made a video showing everyone Randy's house and asking if anyone had a truck to donate.

Late that night, a man from Sevierville named David messaged and said he had a truck. He left his phone number, and I called, even though it was after 9:00 p.m. I was too excited to wait.

David's voice broke when he explained the situation.

"I saw the video," he said. "And I thought I'm one man with two trucks. Why should I not give one of these trucks to bless someone else? The Lord pricked my heart. So I'm driving up there on Friday, and I'm bringing Randy this truck."

My heart was ready to burst. By the time we got off the phone, it was too late to call Randy, and I tossed and turned, talking to God.

My sleepless prayer went something like this: "God, who am I that I get to tell these people they're getting a new truck or a car or a camper or a new house? I'm just not worthy to be part of any of this."

The next morning, I waited as long as I could, which was only until 7:30 a.m. As soon as I dropped off my daughter at school, I called Randy. It rang and rang.

When he finally answered, I was already apologizing. "Randy! I'm so sorry! Am I calling too early?"

He sounded a little tired. "Um, no. You're fine. What is it?"

"I just couldn't wait another minute to tell you!" I squealed. "This guy messaged me last night from Sevierville, and he's donating a truck! God sent you a truck! Our prayers are answered!"

The other end of the line was silent. Finally, Randy's quiet reply came through. "I can't... believe it."

I practically screamed into the phone. "I know! Isn't this amazing? I couldn't wait to tell you!"

Randy remained quiet again for a beat. Then he said, "Courtney, I gotta tell you a story."

"Okay." I was still driving, my grin reaching for my ears.

"Twenty days after the storm hit, I was staying in my house. A volunteer from out of state was staying with me, helping. And this big box came in the mail. Now, it had no return address, but I didn't order it. I don't order things online. I tried to take it to the post office to send it back, but they said there was no way to do that. So I took it home and opened it. And you know what it was?"

"What?"

"It was a truck bed cover."

My mouth dropped. I hiccuped.

Randy continued. "That night, I told the guy staying with me, 'If God sends me a truck now, I'm gonna go out and buy a suit and go back to church. Because I'll know God is real.'"

He sniffed and stopped talking.

Tears spilled down my cheeks.

"And now He's sent me a truck," he whispered.

*

That week, as promised, God's volunteers from Iowa finished the last few repairs and installs at

Jack's house. The framing crew from West Virginia was rebuilding the back half of Frank and Mindy's. We also had the Kentucky guys framing on Clearwater Street.

From my Facebook inbox, I learned someone else from out of state was designing T-shirts to sell and do fundraisers for the work. Another lady from Knoxville was collecting funds through her church. They were bringing a four-thousand-dollar check that week. A man from Roan Mountain was driving down to Hampton to make barbecue for the framing crews and the Iowa guys too.

Each of these individuals represented a unique member of the Lord's body, all with different talents and motives. But God was drawing every part together, working them where needed, to shine His light and bring revival, to spread His love to a hurting and scattered community.

It made me think of the verse in I Corinthians 12:4–5: "Now there are varieties of gifts, but the same Spirit; and there are varieties of service, but the same Lord."

That Friday, January 31, David from Sevierville rolled into town hauling Randy's truck. Our Iowa volunteers came over from Jack's house to watch the exchange.

"Now there's something else I want to explain about this truck," David said to Randy as soon as they'd unloaded it off the trailer. Teary-eyed, he rested one hand on the toolbox in the back. "The tools in this box belonged to my dad. He recently passed away. After I heard about your situation, I decided to include my dad's tools too—because I can think of no better way to honor his memory than to pass these along to you."

Randy cried. David cried. I cried.

And even though the forecast that morning had predicted nonstop buckets of rain all day, the clouds parted, and the sun beamed down on us against a vibrant blue sky. Randy shook hands with David and thanked him again.

I relayed Randy's "Truck Bed Cover" story on Facebook that week, and dozens of Christians reached out wanting to buy him a suit. By the next week, along with the items on his Amazon wish list, he had half a dozen new suits hanging in his closet.

CHAPTER NINETEEN

We had nearly every item needed to rebuild Frank and Mindy's house. And it was only February 2.

"So we won't have to use much of the church funds?" Paul asked me.

I ticked off items in my notebook. "Siding and donated windows are scheduled to arrive February 10." I chewed on the end of my pen and smiled. "That's pretty ironic, considering that's the day our twenty-three volunteers arrive."

"That's not ironic. That's God," Paul corrected me.

I nodded, and peaceful assurance flooded my heart.

At this point, why even try lining up building materials or labor? God was driving this ministry while I reclined in the passenger seat, watching in awe as His progress zipped past my window.

*

February 2, I received a message from a man in Arkansas. He explained he'd been refurbishing a classic Jeep, which he wanted to donate to Frank. Frank's truck had washed across his yard during the flood and ended up standing on its end, halfway up a tree.

I messaged Frank about the Jeep, but he insisted he didn't need it. He hated to ask for help or accept charity. Someone had given him a car for the time being, and he was just fine if we wanted to pass along the blessing to someone else. I shrugged it off, assuming God had a better plan. But in the meantime, I forgot to message our donor from Arkansas and tell him. The days were long and jumbled. It was my honest mistake.

On February 10, as scheduled, our first wave of thirteen volunteers arrived from Illinois, Kentucky, and Pennsylvania. Ten more were scheduled to arrive the following day. The first team jumped in to work right away, some of them having driven over twelve hours to spend their entire week working with us. They were staying at Doe River Gorge, and their goal for the week was to complete siding, roofing, insulation, and drywall at Frank and Mindy's, plus flooring at another home.

That day, someone from North Carolina messaged to let me know their family had purchased the six-hundred-dollar weed trimmer on Randy's Amazon wish list. For some reason, that particular item couldn't be shipped. So this family did their research and found the same piece of equipment at an Ace Hardware thirty minutes away. I agreed to pick it up and make the delivery to Randy. The best part? He had no idea.

When I walked into Ace Hardware that morning and explained why I was there, the guys behind the counter just gawked like I'd grown two heads. Perhaps I was a bit emotional and excited.

"So you're here to pick up a... trimmer... that someone bought... from North Carolina?" one of them asked.

"Yes!" I couldn't stop smiling.

My new friend wasn't amused. In fact, he might've thought I was scamming them.

"Hang on. Let me go look in the back."

The other employee behind the counter spoke up when he walked away. "I think I remember the piece of equipment you're talking about. Someone called yesterday from Monroe, North Carolina, and said they wanted to buy it, that this lady would be picking it up." He reached for an invoice under the counter. "Are you Courtney Dailey?"

"Yes, I am!"

"It's back here." The man moved past me as his fellow employee returned.

"God is rebuilding flood-damaged homes in the Hampton and Valley Forge areas," I explained to both men. "We're on our seventh house, and people from all over the world are helping us rebuild and sending the things people need to get back in their homes."

They both stopped what they were doing and stared at me. Maybe because I was crying? It happened on a regular basis. Every day, in fact, if not multiple times a day. I couldn't help it.

The man behind the counter finally smiled, and his eyes softened. "You mean those people from North Carolina have never met you and they've never met the guy getting this string trimmer?"

I nodded my head. "That's right."

The other guy chimed in. "That's a six-hundred-dollar piece of equipment."

They shared a glance.

"I know. It's all of God's family, coming together to show love and help others."

The man behind the counter blinked. "Wow." He rubbed his chin, silent for a beat. "Well, God bless you for doing this."

"Oh, it's not me." I held up my hand in a stop gesture. "It's God. God's the one doing this."

All the way to my car, I cried and prayed in the parking lot. God wasn't just using this flood to impact the flood survivors, the volunteers, and the donors. Now, He was using this tragedy as an opportunity to share His light and His will with the guys in Ace Hardware. Because that generous family in North Carolina had donated their money and efforts to bless someone else that morning, God was getting the glory. Two random strangers got an earful about Jesus before it was even time to break for lunch.

When I delivered Randy's weed trimmer that morning, his mom was visiting, sitting in his living room recliner. She pulled me into a hug and cried. She said she couldn't believe the impact of this tragedy on Randy's spiritual life and hers. And we remarked together about how this was the clearest picture of what God's church should always do, showing His love. It was a shame it took a tragedy like this to bring us together to talk to our neighbors and lend a hand.

I left Randy's house thinking once again, who was I to be part of this movement?

*

Two days later, a couple drove in from Knoxville, Tennessee, and met me at our church. This couple had come to check out the work on Jerry's house early on, after the flood. Then they'd gone back home to see if they could do some fundraising for the efforts. To my understanding, they were bringing a four-thousand-dollar check.

"Well, in the last four weeks our little church has been very excited about raising money for this work." The lady hugged me. We were standing with Lori in our church's fellowship hall.

"When you say 'little church,'" I interrupted. "How many members do you have?"

"Well, we had about ninety last month, and most of us are elderly. We can't do much anymore. But we can fundraise."

"That's awesome! Thank you so much for doing this!"

"Oh, thank you. It's been such a blessing to be a part of this work. It got our little congregation excited again. Would you believe we gained eight new members while we were out raising money and talking to people about what's happening here?"

"Eight new members?" I balked.

"Yes! And then there's this." She reached into her pocketbook and handed me an envelope. "We didn't just raise four thousand. We raised ten."

I glanced at Lori, our church secretary. She beamed, her eyes wet. God is so good.

CHAPTER TWENTY

"Hey, Miss Courtney. How are you?" the voice on the other end of the line asked.

I pushed away from my computer screen and took off my glasses, standing to stretch. It was Michael Marcum, the minister from the church in Kentucky, but something in his tone wasn't quite right.

"Michael, I am great. How are you?"

"Well, not so great. That's why I'm calling. Have you seen the news about the floods in Kentucky?"

"Yes." I sank down in my desk chair, heart pounding.

"That was our area."

"Michael..." I put my hand over my mouth. I had no idea.

"Yeah. It's bad. It's every bit as bad as the flood from Hurricane Helene. Maybe worse."

I squeezed the bridge of my nose and closed my eyes.

"Hundreds of homes are gone. People are sleeping in elementary schools or staying in sheds in their yards. We're trying to help as many as we can. But we need you, if possible. I know you're busy."

"Of course I'll help. Yes. Whatever you need. What can I do?"

As soon as we got off the phone, Michael sent photos of their area, and I made a video. Paul and I prayed, and we questioned. Why was this happening? How were the homes on Clearwater Street going to get finished now? It was too much for Michael and Jamie to manage.

Or was it? Had we learned nothing these months? I remembered the verse my mom used to quote when I was a kid, Matthew 19:26b: "...With men this is impossible, but with God all things are possible."

Within twenty-four hours of the video going live, hundreds from God's army gathered supplies and rounded up work crews. I contacted all the local churches who'd been helping with the relief work to collect their leftover blankets, chainsaws, heaters, and generators. Two days later, Michael and Jamie came down with trailers to gather what we'd amassed. Beth began her search for someone who could oversee the homes in Hampton and take over, though Michael insisted it was their commitment and they would see it through.

Our hearts ached for our Kentucky church family, and we prayed diligently. We knew all too well the road ahead of them. As I sorted through messages every day, God sent campers, car leads, and supply leads for Michael, who had also orchestrated a donation link to their church. I shared it with as many as I could.

But amidst the worry and new flurry of activity over our brothers and sisters in Kentucky, I came upon one particular message I'd forgotten. It was from that guy in Arkansas—the one fixing up the Jeep for Frank and Mindy.

Oh no.

He wrote he planned to set out Monday morning, in just four days from the time I was reading the message. He had the Jeep all fixed up and ready. A friend would make the trip with him, and they had it all planned out. My heart plummeted. I'd dropped the ball on this one.

Before I responded, I texted Frank.

Any chance you changed your mind and decided you want that Jeep after all?

He called immediately.

"Hey, Frank. How are you?" I answered.

"I'm good. Listen, it's funny you should send me that message. My car just broke down, and we have no vehicle now. I could sure use that Jeep."

Of course he could.

*

The next day, we organized a paint party at Frank and Mindy's. Standing in the middle of their house that morning, no one would believe it had gone from a half house, studs only, to interior paint ready in a little over three weeks. It had walls. Siding. Drywall. A new roof. Foundation repair. Like I said, this home was moving along on God's timeline, not ours.

One lady who came to paint had driven all the way from Florida the night before, over a nine-hour trip. She was seventy-one years old.

"So you got my message last night that our paint day was today, and you just jumped in your car and drove?" I couldn't help shaking my head.

She shrugged. "It was fine. When I got tired, I stopped at a rest area and slept in my car."

I stared at this strong spitfire. "So where are you staying tonight?"

She kept painting while we talked. "Oh. I'll just find a parking spot somewhere. It's fine."

After painting all day, I insisted she come home with me and stay at our house. My entire family loved her.

*

Four days later, our Arkansas friends met Frank and Mindy in the Big Lots parking lot in Elizabethton to deliver a shiny, refurbished Jeep.

Even Frank cried.

The day after that, Dan came in from Mississippi with Shane, Cody, and Tanner. They were installing gorgeous custom kitchen cabinets and trim work at Frank and Mindy's, plus hanging the cabinets and doing trim at another house. I met them on the jobsite around nine that morning.

They parked their massive trailers in Frank and Mindy's front yard and began unloading cabinets, not wasting a minute. Their craftsmanship was unmatched. Once the materials were unloaded, we circled up in the living room to share our latest God stories and have prayer together.

"I have to tell you a story," Dan said. The guys all looked at each other knowingly, so this must be something big.

Dan's eyes were already full when he began. "I almost died fifteen years ago. My esophagus detached from my stomach, and I went through an extensive surgery and a long hospital stay. I wasn't supposed to live. But God delivered me. It was a long recovery, but I had an ICU nurse praying over me every day. She still says I'm the only patient she's ever seen to survive that.

"Once I was home, I found out I'd racked up a hundred grand in hospital bills. And for fifteen years now, I've been making payments toward that bill. Eighty or more dollars a month. Every month."

"That's a lot. I'm so sorry," I said.

Dan winked. "Oh, just wait, girl. Our God is so good." He sniffed. "So after we delivered the camper up here in December and we left Bumpus Cove, we felt so blessed. It was incredible being here to serve, loving on people. The day after we got home, I got a call from the hospital."

I raised my eyebrows. "Okay?"

"They told me I didn't have to pay anymore."

"What?"

Dan held up a hand, and his family members smiled.

"What do you mean?" I asked.

"That's what I said! I told them I still owed somewhere over eighty grand. And they told me no. These were the exact words they used, 'The debt has been forgiven.'"

"Um. That's not a thing." My throat thickened, closing over my words. "That doesn't happen. Who paid the bill?"

"Girl, you know who took care of that bill."

Dan couldn't outgive God.

My head spun, trying to imagine what it would feel like if someone called me and told me a huge debt had been wiped clean. And then I sobered, because that's what had happened to me. And to all of us.

"And you, who were dead in your trespasses and the uncircumcision of your flesh, God made alive together with Him, having forgiven us all our trespasses, by CANCELING THE RECORD OF DEBT that stood against us with its legal demands. This He set aside, nailing it to the cross" (Colossians 2:13–14).

My debt was nailed to the cross. For five months, we stood in awe of God's miracles, our mouths agape, our cheeks wet. We'd witnessed building materials appearing at just the right time or a well-suited carpenter walking onto the scene in the exact moment we needed him. We'd watched flood survivors get brand-new cars, campers, furniture, and home repair from all over the world, from God's family.

Yet the greatest miracle, beyond anything we'd seen, was still the miracle of eternal life, that precious gift we were granted when Christ died for us. It was the reason I was healed and the reason I got out of bed every morning. I had hope beyond this world with its hospital bills and hurricanes and discouragement.

My debt was forgiven.

CHAPTER TWENTY-ONE

On March 1, our church organized a day trip to the flooded areas of Kentucky. We set up in a church parking lot to pass out hot meals and supplies. I drove separately with just my daughter so we could tour the area with Jamie and make videos for Meades Branch Freewill Baptist Church. They had committed to rebuilding four homes, even before the funds or supplies were provided. In the last five months, I'd watched God repeatedly reward that kind of faith.

The tragedies I witnessed from my single day in Kentucky still haunt me. In the crowd at the church parking lot, some of the folks in line were barefoot, though temps were in the midforties. I met one family living in their shed at the corner of their property. I visited with two other homeowners in their yards as we watched their homes torn down, the fragments loaded into dump trucks. Jamie showed me four different homesites where they were helping families rebuild.

Belongings were piled on roadsides. Someone's fishing cooler was suspended fifty feet in the air from a tree branch. That's how high the waters had risen. Flood victims, their clothing painted in mud, hauled belongings to the curb in wheelbarrows. Their treasures were left for garbage pickup. And there were no disaster-relief vehicles or church vans in sight. It was only the locals doing the best they could with the little bit they had.

That night, after I arrived home, my mind reeled. I couldn't stop crying. My husband listened as I ranted about the day, the destruction I'd witnessed, and my take on how overwhelmed our friends in Kentucky must be. Michael and Jamie had already taken on so much. And now this?

My husband didn't say much. He just listened, like he always does. And when I finished spewing my tears and frustrations, he led us in our nightly prayer.

"Dear God, please be with Courtney and help her understand she is one person and You don't expect her to try to save the whole world."

I raised my head and looked at him.

His eyes remained closed as his prayer continued. "God, You know what these people need. You continue to bless us and do Your will. We're just asking You do the same thing in Kentucky You've done for us here. And please give us the strength to finish the tasks You've laid out for us."

As he prayed, a familiar peace spread through my soul, warming me all over. I understood. I'd fallen into the same trap again: thinking this was somehow my burden, that I needed to take on these additional projects in another state, over three hours from home, on top of the things we were already doing to rebuild in our area.

This was God's project. Not mine. It was His blueprint, and He would provide what was needed. God didn't expect me to do anything but take the next step—or keep riding along in the passenger seat, as it were.

Seven days later, Jamie texted with an immediate need for three more campers. So I went to my Facebook inbox. And you know the rest. Three campers were waiting there for me from Alabama, Florida, and Wisconsin.

I texted him back: *Guess how many campers I found in my inbox!*

He responded: *Three. I know. I figured they were already there. That's why I messaged you to go ahead and check.*

Jamie and Michael had witnessed God's miraculous provisions too. And we all knew. This had nothing to do with me. Or Jamie. Or Meades Branch. Or Central Community Christian Church. It was fully a God thing.

That same week, some of the homeowners we'd helped who were already back in their homes decided to do what they could for our Kentucky friends. They organized trailer loads of supplies, some of them donating the very kerosene heaters Meades Branch brought in October. Jeff and Christine donated the car that had been donated for them, paying it forward in a tidy full circle that blessed everyone.

CHAPTER TWENTY-TWO

The second week of March, volunteers named Eugene and Darcy Washburn drove up from south Florida to work on one of the homes and finish difficult trim on doorways, plus do appliance installation. Again, it was the punch-list stuff no one wanted to tackle. We'd first met this couple while finishing the flooring on Jerry's house. They'd rolled onto the jobsite with their daughter, and the three of them were a powerhouse of productivity. They flipped and remodeled homes for a living and decided to put their talents to work for the Lord.

To say we were grateful for our volunteers is a gross understatement.

By the time the Washburns returned for a second trip in March, after many calls and texts and over-the-phone prayers, they'd become family.

They stayed at our house, and we shared meals, stories, and prayer time together. I cried and told them I loved them the day they left. They told me I was their new adopted daughter.

This was one more blessing of the work: meeting these brothers and sisters from all over the world. We weren't strangers. Most of the volunteers felt instantly like family. There was a deeper bond—a connection in Christ that wove our spirits together.

"So then you are no longer strangers and aliens, but you are fellow citizens with the saints and members of the household of God" (Ephesians 2:19).

*

The third week of March, a man named Peter arrived from the coast of North Carolina. He was on a mission to finish the last few projects for Frank and Mindy's house. Another answer to prayers. We still needed their microwave mounted, appliances installed, light fixtures put in, and the kitchen sink set up. It was the same last-two-weeks stuff that always fell between the cracks. But God had sent us the perfect person for the job, once again.

Peter rolled into town early on March 18, and I told him we could meet at another house first so I could show him the remaining projects there too.

Ten minutes into my explanation of our biggest priorities, he folded his hands in front of him and gave me a fatherly look. "Young lady, I need you to listen to me about something."

I straightened up. "Yes, sir?"

"You should not be coming down here by yourself to meet a stranger who comes in from out of town to help."

"I know. And I don't usually—"

He held up one hand. "Well, you did today, and I'm just telling you. Don't do it again."

I nodded and swallowed. "Yes, sir."

Peter had such a servant heart. And like with so many of the other volunteers who came into our area, I loved him instantly.

"We are so blessed to have you here," I told him the next day. We were standing next to my car in front of Frank and Mindy's house.

"Oh, I'm the blessed one," he said. "It brings me so much joy to serve these people. While I work on their house, I spend that time in prayer for them."

"I love that. What a wonderful idea."

"It does me good. Especially today."

I raised my eyebrows.

He hesitated, then finally explained, "My divorce is final today."

"Peter! I'm so sorry! That's terrible!"

He rubbed the back of his neck. "It could have been a bad week. Instead, it's wonderful because I'm here focusing on God and serving others."

As I drove home, I replayed his words in my head. Peter was using what could have been the hardest week of his life and turning it into a blessing for someone else. Rather than licking his wounds or wallowing in his own suffering, he was shining brighter. Such a testimony.

*

By April 7, Frank and Mindy's home was complete. We posted their Amazon wish list and helped them with living room and bedroom furniture from a local place just up the road. Here's the crazy part:

God started their house on January 29. It took sixty-eight days to rip off the entire back half of their home, gut everything, and do the foundation repair, all new framing, flooring, roofing, and siding, the electrical and plumbing, plus insulation and drywall, a new kitchen and bathroom, painting, and light fixtures. Sixty-eight days.

Only God.

In April, we picked up smaller needs on two more homes from the next road over. One was an elderly couple who needed a replacement garage door for the one that had washed away. Curtis had already been helping this couple for months, replacing the drywall and flooring and installing a new kitchen. Then another elderly couple needed their hardwood floors resanded. They'd taken on eight inches of water during the flood.

The day after we committed to helping both families, someone reached out to me on Facebook and asked for the exact cost of the garage door so they could make a donation to our church. April 19, a man contacted Curtis about refinishing the floors in the second house. He told him it would be June before he could get to it, but that the estimate for the labor and materials was zero dollars.

The text thread for our Valley Forge relief work was just... insane. There were no words for it. There were so many projects happening at once. We were coordinating invoices to be paid and which crews were working at which house on what day. And then every so often, someone would post a problem or an issue.

One time, Curtis texted all of us and said he was having major holdups with the toilet install in one house. He was trying to finish the last few things to get this lady moved back in. But he was wondering if something was defective on the toilet, and he wasn't sure what to do.

We started looking for a replacement toilet. So many donations remained in the storage container at church and in different houses with ongoing work projects.

Exactly twelve minutes later, Curtis texted again: *Disregard the last message. God's way ahead of me.*

We didn't even ask him why or how, which might seem strange. But by that point in the relief work, we all knew. There were hundreds of instances where we threw our hands in the air, wondering how to remedy a crisis, not knowing God had the solution worked out. We just needed to wait a few more minutes for Him to show us the way.

Keith and Curtis were also installing kitchen cabinets for another couple, Alan and Bonnie, who lived near Randy. This home project had been ongoing since shortly after the flood, but progress was slow. The water had risen three or four feet in their house and washed away their vehicle. Alan's shed was gone too.

They'd lost everything but the shell of their home and didn't know for many months if it could be repaired or would have to be torn down. They had flood insurance, so they were paying the trades to do repairs out of pocket. Our volunteers helped where they could, but we reserved the flood-relief funds for folks who didn't have a backup.

Ironically enough, the homes with no government or insurance help were repaired and built back at lightning speed, compared to the folks who had to wait on insurance adjusters or organizations. After seven months, Alan and Bonnie's house was finally painted inside, and flooring was installed. I showed them how to set up their Amazon wish list so they could make preparations to move back in. It had been a long, cold winter.

"Right after the flood, we were trying to decide if we needed to rent or what we were going to do," Alan told me. "Obviously, we couldn't stay in the house. A member of our church was here in our driveway, and I asked him if he had any ideas. That's when his phone rang." Alan raised one eyebrow.

I could only nod, grinning, because I already knew what he would say.

"The man on the phone was someone he didn't know, from Knoxville. He didn't even know how he got his number. But the man was asking if he could donate a camper to someone in need. I was standing right there in front of him."

The gorgeous fifth-wheel camper was hauled in right away. Alan and Bonnie had been living in the camper in their driveway for seven months since that day. Now, though the title had been signed over to them, they wanted to pay it forward and bless someone else with the camper. He told me to be on the lookout if I heard of a need.

*

The home just down from Frank and Mindy's was finished near the end of April, and that homeowner was also able to make an Amazon wish list of her needs. Per the norm, she was flooded with boxes of household items and messages from strangers all over the world in just forty-eight hours. She was a grandmother, the matriarch of her family who always took care of others. Another church was setting a new trailer for her nephew next door. And just down the street, other churches were setting up two new trailers for more flood victims.

*

The third week of April, Jamie called. We loved hearing the God stories from our Kentucky brothers. They had front-row seats to God's miracles and provisions in their devastated area.

"Are you sitting down?" he asked. "I can't wait to share this one with you."

I sat at my kitchen table. "Now I am."

"So last week, Michael was down there working on the houses in Hampton, and he went to a meeting with a bunch of the area coordinators. While he was there, everyone got started talking and telling their stories. He was telling about how we were about to start our new church building before this flood hit, but then we put the plans on hold to help rebuild in Tennessee."

"Yes! I remember that!"

"Well, after the meeting, this lady comes up to Michael and says, 'You put your new church build on hold to help people?' After he confirmed that, she says, 'Well, I'm with the Mississippi Nailbenders. Have you ever heard of them?' He hadn't, of course, but then she went on to tell him how they pick a charitable project to do every single year. It's this huge group of hundreds of contractors and carpenters from all over the United States.

They line up their workdays with a specific project in mind."

"For real?"

"Yeah. And get this. They were supposed to rebuild a home for a flood victim, but the project fell through. That's why she was in Hampton." The line went silent for a moment. "So they have hundreds of workers lined up, who took time off work and were planning to come help, starting May 26. But now they have nowhere for them to go."

I folded my hands on the table in front of me and whispered, "No way."

"The next day, the president of Mississippi Nailbenders calls Michael and tells him they want to build our entire church! They start in a few weeks."

We giggled and cried and praised God together. Because this little church had stepped out in faith and decided to help others, sacrificing their agenda, God took care of their needs. He sent hundreds from His army to build their beautiful new church building while they were still working in the trenches.

"We gotta start demo on the old church building. Like, tomorrow." Jamie laughed.

And this is the verse that came to mind: "Give, and it will be given to you. Good measure, pressed down, shaken together, running over, will be put into your lap. For with the measure you use it will be measured back to you" (Luke 6:38).

CHAPTER TWENTY-THREE

In May, we hired a man to come in and repair a driveway for our biggest project yet: Charlie's house. He needed a complete teardown and rebuild. The first day I went out to look at his property, I was blown away. His driveway was the last outlet of a dead-end road, a steep, muddy drop-off winding into the woods and out of sight. I couldn't get my car back in there, not with the washout so awful. So I walked in on foot.

As I emerged into the clearing at the bottom of the driveway, it was like going back in time. The river ran right along Charlie's front yard. Towering mountains framed flowering trees in bloom. No other houses stood in sight. Just the sound of white water and the smell of crisp mountain air. It was a beautiful oasis.

And there sat Charlie's house, right in the middle of it.

The water had risen about four feet in his home. The whole back half of the structure was sinking, its foundation destroyed and the walls buckling. If there was any chance of hauling in equipment to demo the house and deliver lumber for the new build, we had to get his driveway repaired. We must also adhere to the new postflood guidelines about base ground elevation. When we rebuilt the house, we'd have to move it to higher ground next to his current lot and set it up on blocks.

Charlie was thrilled for the help. He didn't care what we had to do, and he wasn't picky. He was just eager to get back into a home. His grandparents had built the house and formed the very foundation from river rocks. Even the stone chimney was built with river rock. Charlie asked if we could save that part of the house at least, so he could make an outdoor fireplace next to the new home.

By May 12, the driveway was repaired, and we needed a demo crew. I was sitting at our store, working in my office. It was a stressful day, running numbers and ordering inventory. Our store still wasn't doing well, and I'd panicked about it for months now. Would I never learn to trust God fully, even after all He'd shown me?

I leaned back in my chair to take a break. Then I felt a nudge. For no reason whatsoever, I opened my Facebook Messenger app. I was weeks behind, and I always checked the messages in order of the oldest first. But today, as I opened my messages, the most recent message showed a preview at the top of the screen.

The first few words of the message clear: *Do you need a demo crew?*

It was the only message I read.

I clicked on it. The inquiry was from a Florida man who owned a demolition company. He said he'd felt God tugging on him to come, and now was his chance. This was his area of expertise. He left his number, and I called him.

"I've been wanting to come help for months," he admitted. "But I had a bad fall and injured my shoulder. So I was delayed until it healed."

He was delayed until the week we needed his particular skill for this particular job.

*

Days later, our texting thread discussed the needs for Charlie's house. Someone was donating appliances. Someone else had lumber, subfloor, and insulation. Another donor was talking to their crew about raising money for windows and roofing. Our Mississippi guys had committed to doing his kitchen cabinets, trim, and interior doors. We had almost everything we needed, and donations were still on the rise.

"I doubt we'll have to use many of the church's flood-relief funds on this one either." I settled at the dining table beside my husband. "But God is still sending money."

It gave me chills all over. The more God sent, the more we knew it could only mean one thing: He wasn't done yet. We couldn't see more than a few feet in front of us, but God saw our path. He knew where this work was headed.

But that afternoon, my husband had come home from work perplexed.

"Something strange happened today, and I can't get it off my mind." He braced his elbows on the table, head in his hands, eyes closed. "I was at the tractor place looking at equipment, and a man was there making a delivery. We struck up a conversation. I don't know why, but the subject turned to the flood. Come to find out, he lives in Jonesborough, and his home was hit hard back in September."

When Paul told me the man's location, I gulped. It was near Bumpus Cove. We'd seen some of that area firsthand—the treeless, bare land, where many homes were swept away.

"Did he lose everything?" I touched Paul's arm.

"Pretty much." He shifted his chair to face me. "He had some farm equipment and vehicles, plus he lost most of his house. The water was eight feet deep inside their house. His insurance only covered the vehicles, so he took that money and used it to start building back his house on his own. He's in his sixties. After working for seven months, in between working his full-time job, he has the home to where he and his wife can live in the upstairs."

"How has he managed it?"

"Well, he said he had some muck-out crews come through to help early on. Then another organization helped some. But mostly, he's been on his own. This local home supply warehouse down there knows the situation. So they've been letting him charge what he needs."

"Just charge his building supplies to the company? How's he going to pay it back?"

Paul pressed his lips together. "I don't know. He said they hadn't worked out a payment plan. The owners are trusting it will work out, and he is too."

I bit my lip. "How much does he owe?"

"Nineteen thousand." Paul let out a whoosh of air. "I don't know, but it felt like I was supposed to meet him, like we were pushed together in that moment, having that particular conversation because God's nudging us to help him."

I slid onto his lap, my throat closing. I understood. God had arranged dozens of divine appointments for us. It wasn't hard to recognize. Usually, the hair on my arms would stand up, and

I'd get a lump in my throat, knowing this was the right thing to do.

"So I went ahead and called that building supply warehouse." Paul's arms settled around me, his chin resting atop my head. "I just wanted to double-check and see what was happening. Sure enough, the lady who answered confirmed everything the man had told me."

"You think God wants us to use some of the flood-relief funds to pay his bill at the building supply place?"

Paul held me tighter. "I do."

After we brought it before the rebuilding crew, everyone agreed. This was the reason these funds were given. We didn't want to have multiple meetings and second-guess what we were supposed to do. Every time we stepped out to answer a call or fulfill a need, God replenished the funds. Just the week before, a church from Maryville had sent over twelve grand.

Lori printed a check from the flood-relief fund, and Paul took it to the building supply company that week. The flood victim called him, choked up.

"I just knew God was telling me to go talk to you that day." His voice cracked. "He was looking out for me."

"Yes, He was," my husband confirmed. "This is nothing we're doing, brother. This is all God's work."

*

June 7, our volunteer from Florida came in to demo Charlie's house. His equipment didn't arrive as planned. He was only going to stay one day but ended up working from dawn until dark for a solid week.

A few days into the demo work, I stopped by Charlie's property to bring our demo guy bottled water and see how things were going.

I had to yell over the machinery to get his attention. He was making piles of what remained from Charlie's house. When he cut the engine, I handed him the cold waters, and the only sound was the white water from the river and the birds chirping. Gnats swarmed our faces. The air smelled like earth.

"There's so much more to do than I realized." He wiped his forehead on the shoulder of his dirty T-shirt. "I'm going to repair the road too, and I'd like to get the pad ready for the house. I can clear out some brush and things."

"That would be wonderful!" I propped one rubber boot on the tread of his excavator. "I can't tell you how much we appreciate you."

"This is such a good feeling." The rims of his eyes were red. "To be here and help someone like this is just incredible."

I could only nod, smiling. This was the greatest part of my day too—leaving the stress of work and the cares of the world and heading down into the Valley Forge area to see what God was doing. To stand on those jobsites witnessing His miracles was to stand at His throne and sing praises. It was a time of worship and perspective.

While we stood there, the dumpster truck showed up and backed down the hill. The driver had been assigned to work at Charlie's for the day, hauling dumpsters every time our volunteer filled one. After he backed in, he hopped out of the truck and walked over to us.

"Is this your home?" he asked me.

"No, sir. Not at all. I'm just here to help coordinate efforts. God's been rebuilding homes through our church for the last nine months. This is the fifteenth home."

The man's eyes widened. "Fifteenth?"

"Yes, sir! And every time we take on a new home, God sends every single thing we need. He provides all the materials to make it happen. We really just sit back and watch at this point."

"Well, what do you still need for this house? Do you have the kitchen covered?"

"We have all of the appliances and the kitchen cabinets donated. We're pretty much covered there..." I chewed my lip. "Except for the countertops."

The man smiled. "That's what I do."

Of course he did.

"I'm a minister," he went on to explain. "We are actually going to South Dakota with a team this summer, and that's all we're doing: installing kitchen countertops for multiple homes on a reservation. I can help with the countertops."

I swallowed back the tears. "Can I please get your name and phone number?"

The volunteer demo guy from Florida just smiled, his eyes filling with tears.

After the dumpster delivery guy left, I clapped. "What are the odds the dumpster delivery guy who shows up here in the few minutes I'm here is the guy who specializes in countertops, the one thing we still needed for Charlie's kitchen?"

Then we both laughed through our tears, standing in awe of one more miracle. One more day. One more house. One more soul touched. All to the glory of God.

When our volunteer left, headed for New York, he said he wanted to stop through again in a couple of months to check the progress and work with us on his way back to Florida. And as we said our goodbyes, he handed us an envelope. It was a donation of twenty-five hundred dollars toward Charlie's house, five hundred toward our building fund at our church, and another thousand toward our church's food route.

CHAPTER TWENTY-FOUR

The second week of June, our church was doing
Vacation Bible School. The coordinator asked me to
make videos of Charlie's home project, so the kids
could do a fundraiser.

"What else do you need to raise money for on
Charlie's house?" she asked as we stood in the
church foyer after services.

I frowned. "Honestly, I couldn't tell you. I think
God has it covered."

"Well, the kids want to help."

"Okay," I agreed. "I'll make some videos about
Charlie's story."

After all, when we were done with Charlie's,
who knew what God had planned next? The kids
raised quite a bit of money that week. One little girl

from church, just six years old, gave a one-hundred-dollar bill from her piggy bank to help him.

The next week, a volunteer agreed to take down some trees on Charlie's land where we were planning to rebuild the house. He wasn't charging us a dime.

*

One night, while checking Facebook messages, I came across a lady in Roan Mountain. She asked if there was any way we could help her neighbor. He was living in a camper before the flood, but the storm had destroyed it. Now he'd been living in a shed for nine months and needed help.

I texted Alan and Bonnie, asking if they'd found a home for their camper. Alan told me it was going to a family who had lost their home in a fire. I got out my phone to make a Facebook video, to see if anyone out there could send this man a camper. I was halfway through recording the video when Alan's number popped up on my screen. I stopped the recording and answered.

"Courtney, do you still need this camper?"

"Yes!"

"Another camper was donated for that family with the house fire. You can have ours."

The next day, I took my teenage son with me up to Roan Mountain to find the man in the shed. I wanted to make sure the need was legitimate and check out the property, to work out some logistics before we scheduled the camper delivery. I pulled up at the address and parked before a single-wide trailer. Right next to the driveway was a shed built from rusty tin. The door didn't close all the way, exposing lawn equipment and other items stored inside, and plants were taking over, growing into gaps in the sides.

Right in the middle of the shed was a filthy, worn mattress and a cooler with a can of peanut butter on top. A flannel shirt hung on a rusty nail in the doorway.

A man sat out front in a camping chair.

"Are you Mason?" I approached.

"No, but I'll get him." He pushed up from his seat.

My son and I stood there in the yard, staring at the unthinkable, while we waited for the man to bring back Mason. It was hard not to stare when Mason walked up. He was covered in bug bites, sores, and dirt. He must've been about sixty years old. Insects were crawling in an open wound on one of his swollen feet. He was shuffling through the dirt in house slippers.

I cleared my throat. "Mason?"

"Yeah. That's me." He scratched at his arm.

"Hi. I'm the one your neighbor told you about. My name is Courtney. I came by to meet you today and show you a picture of the camper God is giving you."

He wouldn't raise his gaze from the ground. "I can't do it today. I'm about to get a ride to the doctor. I have some new whelps that came up on me today, and I don't know what they are."

I swallowed and tried not to stare at the sores on his arms. "Okay. I understand. We have to find someone to haul it, but then we'll be bringing you a new home."

I followed him over to the doorway of the shed, and he showed me the inside.

"How have you managed living in here for nine months?" I asked.

He shrugged. "It wasn't so bad. I don't like to ask for help. Sometimes I would sleep on my sister's couch if it got real cold. Or I'd come out here in the yard and build a fire. The worst part has been the bugs, and the dogs that would come in the shed at night." Mason chuckled, like it was no big deal.

"Well, we're here to help. Do you have a phone? Can I call you?"

"Don't have a phone."

"Okay. I'll send a message by your neighbor on the day we're bringing the camper. Okay?"

He still wouldn't make eye contact with me. "Sounds good."

When I showed him the picture of the massive, state-of-the-art camper, his eyes lit up. I honestly believe he would have been thrilled to have the camper with no sewer hookup or even electricity, just to get a roof over his head.

By the time I left Mason's property, my head was lost in a giant brainstorm, trying to think of everything he would need. Bedding and blankets.

Clothing and shoes. Groceries and dishes. Pots and pans. A microwave and medical supplies.

I called Alan on my way back down the mountain.

"Alan, can you give me a list of everything you guys left in the camper, so I can get supplies together for Mason?"

"We fully stocked it," he said. "Bonnie washed all the bedding. Plus, there are blankets. Pillows. Dishes. Pots and pans. Some groceries. We left a toaster oven. There's even shampoo, conditioner, cleaning supplies, towels."

Right. Of course there was. The only things we needed to pick up for Mason were clothes, some more groceries, medical supplies, and a Bible.

Because more than giving Mason a dry and safe place to sleep, the physical things he needed, the greatest gift we could give him was the promise of a perfect life beyond this earth. We wanted to show him God's love.

Jerry worked day and night finding someone who could haul the camper. It was delivered two days later. And the day after that, we were able to bring in more supplies to meet Mason's every need. God had provided. Once again.

CHAPTER TWENTY-FIVE

It feels incomplete that this is the last chapter of my God Stories book. As these accounts come to a close, the work does not. As I type this, it is the first week of July. We are about to stake out Charlie's house and dig footers. Keith has already found another family in Roan Mountain who needs a complete teardown and rebuild. If it's God's will, that project will be our sixteenth family God has helped through our church (not including all the other churches in the area and what they have done through God's provisions). As the funds and work crews still pile up by the hundreds in my Facebook inbox and I now fall seven weeks behind on my replies, I stand in awe. A constant lump in my throat.

Because it never gets old, watching God move.

Our work here is nowhere near done. And the stories included in this book don't cover half the miracles we've witnessed over the last nine months. My dear friends, our God is alive. He came in after the storm and dried our tears with His mercy.

But more than the lumber or the trailer underpinning or the Lowe's gift cards, God supplied hope. He brought revival to a depleted community and joined the hands of brothers and sisters who once stood divided. He showed His miracles to the people on social media who were struggling in their faith or facing physical or financial hardships. He used this tragedy as a healing balm.

Throughout this ministry, my weaknesses have been magnified. I've been made small, staring in wonder at our powerful, almighty God who listens to our every prayer and answers. He shines His blessings and stands by His promises.

We are His children. And if you aren't a child of God, I would encourage you to read His Word. The Bible can melt your heart and give you the clarity that no other book or human story ever could.

If you picked up this book because you needed your faith strengthened, I encourage you to act on that nudge. Search His Word. Read about the call He has for your life. He wants you to believe in Him and repent of your sins. "For everyone who calls on the name of the Lord will be saved" (Romans 10:13). "Repent therefore, and turn back, that your sins may be blotted out" (Acts 3:19).

If you haven't put on Christ in baptism, now is the time. Don't wait.

He's standing, watching, ready to welcome you into His open arms and His family. He wants *you*. "Repent and be baptized every one of you in the name of Jesus Christ for the forgiveness of your sins, and you will receive the gift of the Holy Spirit" (Acts 2:38).

And when you give your life over to Him, leaning on His guidance and continuing to ask for forgiveness of your sins, the blood of Jesus will continue to cleanse you. "But if we walk in the light, as He is in the light, we have fellowship with one another, and the blood of Jesus His Son cleanses us from all sin" (I John 1:7).

Finally, wherever you are in your spiritual walk, I encourage you to pray and read His Word every day. Look for ways you can reach out to serve others. There's no better feeling and no better gift than to sacrifice your time and talents to someone in need. I think God tells us to do this in Scripture because He knows that's the recipe. His ways are the instruction manual, how to have the happiest life secure in Him.

"As each has received a gift, use it to serve one another, as good stewards of God's varied grace" (I Peter 4:10).

This entire voyage has opened my eyes to so many things I never saw before. But one of the biggest changes in my life has been a new clarity in recognizing God's nudges and His provisions. I was so busy with my world and my to-do list, going about my days, I often forgot to stop and seek ways to make room for the Lord to work in my life and my family. I'm more aware of His blessings now. I see them. And I'm more grateful for those thousands of answered prayers through the years.

God doesn't belong in a box. He made the box. He made everything. He can do anything, and without Him, we are nothing.

In all things, no matter how many homes are built and how many families are helped, the glory belongs to God. When we faltered on every building project, God picked up the slack. When we messed up the plan, He swooped in to repair our mistakes. That's the Sovereign God we serve. And we will forever praise Him for all He's done in this place.

THE END

To see the videos and photos of the full story
and the progress of God's work to date,
be sure and follow Courtney's Facebook page at
Author Courtney Dailey.

Or connect alternatively through:

Instagram: Courtney Dailey Writes
https://www.instagram.com/courtneydaileywrites?igsh=M
WdtdG4yanpicmNxdg==

YouTube: Author Courtney Dailey
https://youtube.com/@authorcourtneydailey?si=tbNf6wF_
AN5o6eQt

Substack: Dailey's Weekly

Website: authorcourtneydailey.com